W9-BHK-142

THE NEW
*Sacher*
COOKBOOK

ALEXANDRA GÜRTLER
CHRISTOPH WAGNER

# THE *Sacher* NEW

# COOKBOOK

FAVORITE AUSTRIAN DISHES

WITH RECIPES BY HANS PETER FINK

IN COLLABORATION WITH
JAROSLAV MÜLLER AND MANFRED STÜFLER

PHOTOGRAPHERS
CHRISTINA MARIA ANZENBERGER-FINK
LUZIA ELLERT AND JOHANNES KITTEL

PICHLER VERLAG

*Sacher*

For their generous support we would like to thank:
"Gastro Rudolf Holzmann", Vienna,
Daniela Birkmayer from
"Rasper & Söhne Nfg GmbH & Co KG", Vienna,
and Hanni Vanicek and Hildegard Michenthaler,
"Zur Schwäbischen Jungfrau" in Vienna.

A special thanks to the following people for their
contributions to the photography of the food:
Sous Chef Thomas Törpel and Chef Saucier Bernd Winkler,
as well as the entire cooking staff of the Sacher Hotel.

ISBN 3-85431-380-2
© 2005 Pichler Verlag, a division of
Styria Pichler Verlag Ltd, Vienna, Austria
*www.styriapichler.at*

*Food stylist:* Hans Peter Fink
*Editorial department and specialist consultant:*
Renate Wagner-Wittula
*Editor:* Olivia Volpini de Maestri
*Translation:* Mỹ Huê McGowran

*Ambiance photos:* Christina Maria Anzenberger-Fink
*Cover photo and chapter title pages:* Luzia Ellert
*Food photographer:* Johannes Kittel

Hotel Sacher archive: p. 8, 9, 13 below right, 48, 61 below

*Cover and book design:* Bruno Wegscheider

*Reproduction:* Pixelstorm, Vienna
*Printed and bound by*
Printing house Theiss Ltd, St. Stefan im Lavanttal

# CONTENTS

Page 6
THE SACHER –
A PIECE OF
VIENNA

Page 76
FISH

Page 24
BREAKFAST
IN HOTEL
SACHER

Page 84
POULTRY

Page 36
CLASSIC
STARTERS

Page 96
MEAT DISHES

Page 42
SACHER'S
FINEST SOUPS &
SOUP GARNISHES

Page 118
COLD
DESSERTS

Page 50
FINE INTERIM
COURSES

Page 136
WARM
DESSERTS

Page 66
SACHER À LA
VÉGÉTARIENNE

Page 161
INDEX

ALL RECIPE INGREDIENTS ARE FOR FOUR SERVINGS

Sacher

THE SACHER –

Pension. Familien Hôtel I. Ranges.
Zimmer v. fl. 1 aufwärts.
Aufzug Bäder

Telephon
Nr. 347

SACHER GARTEN

HOTEL SACHER vis à vis Hof-Oper

Restaurant Ed. Sacher

FASS-ABGTEILER KELLER

K.K. Hof-Weinhandlung

ED. JACOB SACHER k.u.k. Hoflieferant

H. NOBACK, Eisenach.

Wien, am 16. Januar 18

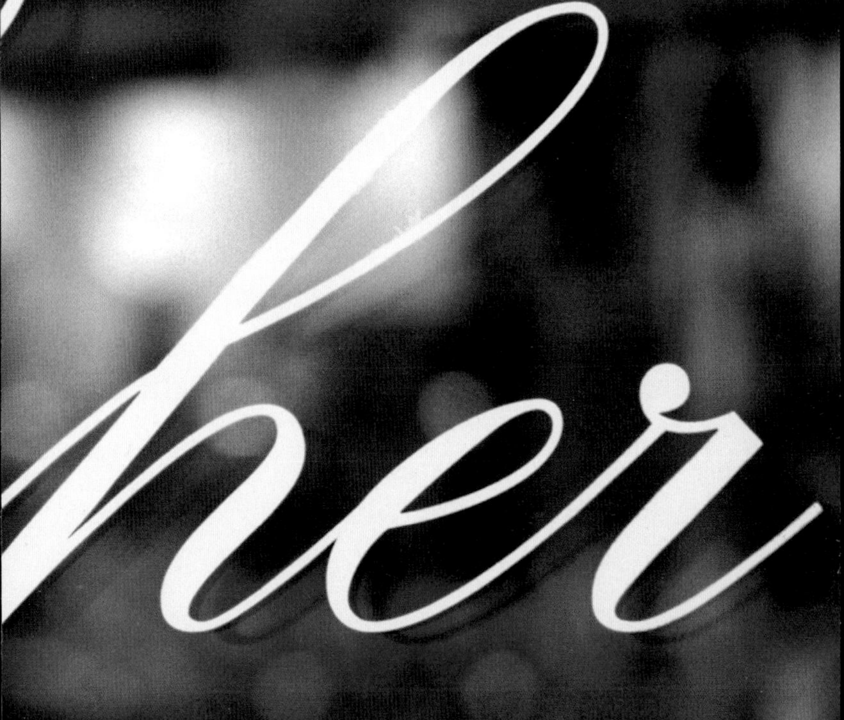

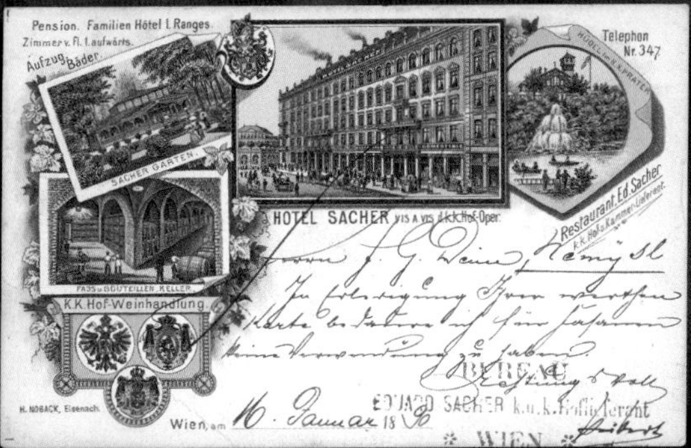

While most established hotels of the world existed before their meals were created, the Sacher Hotel acquired a name for itself precisely the other way around. Here, in the beginning, there existed a dish – namely a cake – and to a certain extent, everything else developed from there.

The cake was created in 1832, long before the hotel existed, by a young man full of hope. Franz Sacher, apprentice cook at the court of the then almost omnipotent Count Metternich, had not only talent, but also good fortune. The count's chef, who came from France, the motherland of grande cuisine, fell ill when a large soirée was planned in the house, for which the state chancellor had ordered a new dessert creation.

Is this where the legend began? Did Franz Sacher simply invent a new chocolate cake? Did he ask his sister for advice? Was he inspired by cake recipes found in the pages of Biedermeier cookbooks?

Anything is possible, and much is speculated. In any case, what is known is this: The count got his cake, and it was a great success. The original Sacher Torte, and with it Franz Sacher, became an indelible part of Austrian identity.

Despite his invention, Franz Sacher did not become famous as a confectioner. Rather, he was one of the greatest cooks of his time, and creator of many success-ful recipes, which contributed to the essence of 'Viennese cuisine'.

Eduard Sacher, son of the creator of the Sacher Torte, continued his father's work as purveyor to the Imperial and Royal court, and opened an elegant hotel – the Hotel Sacher – based on Parisian models, opposite the newly built court opera house.

8

After Eduard Sacher's death, his wife Anna, the daughter of a butcher from Leopoldstadt, took over the hotel's management. The hotel became a favorite meeting place for aristocratic lovers of the Austro-Hungarian monarchy, and in her time, Anna Sacher managed to get aristocrats – even Emperor Franz Josef himself – to sign their names on a large tablecloth (which can still be viewed in the hotel today). "The master of the house is me!" was the motto of the cigar-smoking Anna Sacher. Yet all Anna's charisma couldn't change the fact that, with the downfall of the Austro-Hungarian monarchy and the succession of two world wars, the luxurious Hotel Sacher would have to survive several serious crises.

The leap from the 'sunken epoch' of the bygone beatitude of the grand hotel into the modern-day luxury hotel business is inextricably connected with the name Gürtler, a family that not only introduced electricity into the Sacher Hotel, but also modern business practices.

Beginning in 1962, Peter Gürtler carefully led the Hotel Sacher into the modern age of gastronomy, and also acquired the "Österreichischer Hof" – today's Hotel Sacher Salzburg – as Sacher's sister hotel.

Since Peter Gürtler's death, both businesses have been running under the classical "family-run business" ethos, and belong to the elite category of "leading hotels of the world".

*From left to right: Creator of the cake, Franz Sacher; founder of the hotel, Eduard Sacher; Anna Sacher's famous "tablecloth of prominent figures", with Emperor Franz Josef's signature in the center; hotel legend Anna Sacher, photographed by Madame d'Ora.*

*Sacher*

French star designer Pierre-Yves Rochon's creative talent was employed for the renovation of the Sacher Hotel interior in 2004-2005. Through Rochon's designs the hotel became even grander, and the suites and rooms were transformed to reach the newest level of luxury hotel standards while still keeping the lovable and traditional feeling of the Sacher Hotel.

*The "holy halls" of the Sacher Hotel provide an ideal place to read the newspaper and drink coffee between appointments in the city. The original Sacher Torte is a must for those with a sweet tooth.*

*Sacher*

*World-famous cuisine:
The luxurious restaurant "Anna Sacher" (previous double page) and the "Red Bar" (top right). Hans Peter Fink (below left), the young head chef and Manfred Stüfler, Chef de cuisine of the Hotel Sacher, Salzburg (below right), are more than satisfied with the equipment and technical fittings of their kitchens.*

*Sacher*

# BREAKFAST
# IN HOTEL SACHER

# FRIED EGGS WITH TRUFFLES AND POTATO FRITTERS

## INGREDIENTS

**400 g boiling potatoes · 1 egg for the fritters · 4 eggs for frying
30–40 g fresh black truffles · salt · ground pepper
Oil or butter for frying · 1 Tbsp butter for frying the eggs**

## PREPARATION

Peel the potatoes. Grate them coarsely, and add a little salt. Squeeze lightly to get rid of excess juice. Mix together with the egg, salt and pepper, and form small fritters. In a large frying pan, heat the oil or butter and spoon in 4 fritters. Press flat. Fry golden brown on both sides and set aside on a kitchen paper. Keep warm in the oven at 70 °C.

Heat butter in a pan. Carefully fry the four eggs.

Brush the truffles well with a vegetable brush and cut into fine slices. Place one fritter each on a warmed plate, and put a fried egg on top of each fritter.

Serve with sliced truffles as decoration.

## HOW TO DO SOMEONE
## A LITTLE SERVICE ON NIGHT DUTY

*It almost sounds like an episode penned by the likes of Fritz Eckhardt, but Sacher's head porter, Wolfgang Buchmann, swears that the story is true. One day, he recalls, particularly sweet, very much in-love newly-weds, checked in with him. In the middle of the night, the young man came down to the porter's desk and asked for a single room.*

*"I thought I should take action," recounts Buchmann, and ordered a bouquet of roses to be delivered to the lady's room in the morning, and a bottle of champagne to the young man's.*

*"The next day, they were back together in their double room," recalls the "un-asked" volunteer cupid, and adds: "I charged the roses and champagne to their room, but kept my mouth shut!"*

# BUTTER BRIOCHES

INGREDIENTS for approx. 10–15 small brioches

FOR THE PRE-DOUGH MIXTURE

**100 g fine wheat flour, Type 405 · 75 ml lukewarm milk · 40 g sugar
42 g yeast · flour for dusting**

FOR THE MAIN PASTRY

**90 ml milk · 1 egg · 4 egg whites · 400 g fine wheat flour, Type 405
160 g soft butter
10 g salt · flour for the work surface**

FOR DAUBING

**1 egg whites · 1–2 Tbsps milk**

PREPARATION

Pre-dough mixture

First, sift the flour into a bowl. Dissolve the sugar and yeast in lukewarm milk and stir into the flour. Sprinkle the batter with flour, cover with plastic wrap and leave to rise in a warm place (approx. 25 °C) until it has expanded to double its bulk.

For the main pastry, mix together the egg, egg whites and the milk. Put the dough in a bowl and sift flour over it. Add the egg-milk mixture, and knead. Add the butter gradually and finally, a pinch of salt. Knead the dough (either by hand or on the lowest setting of a blender) for 15–20 minutes until smooth and elastic.

Sprinkle with flour, cover with plastic wrap and leave it to rise for 20–25 minutes. Preheat the oven to 220 °C. Work the dough through thoroughly. Again, cover with plastic wrap and leave it to rise again for 20–25 minutes. Put the dough in a baking tin, sprinkle with some flour, and again cover and leave until it has risen to three-quarters its bulk.

From the mass, now make small mounds or small plaited loaves about 40 g in weight. Whisk the egg whites and milk, and brush over the mounds. Place a tray filled with water on the lowest shelf of the oven. Reduce the temperature to 180 °C. Put the brioches on a baking tray covered with baking paper and bake golden brown for about 12 minutes.

Place the brioches on a cake rack and allow to cool.

BAKING TIME: 12 minutes

BAKING TEMPERATURE: Preheat the oven to 220 °C; then reduce to 180 °C

# WHITE ASPARAGUS
# DRESSED IN HAM

## INGREDIENTS

**12 stalks of white asparagus · 12 slices of processed ham · 1 tomato**
**1 Tbsp zucchini cubes · 1 boiled egg · chopped chervil · walnut oil**
**salt · sugar · butter**
**Marinated field salad as garnish**

## PREPARATION

Prepare a large pot of water with salt, a pinch of sugar and some butter and bring
to boil. Meanwhile, peel the asparagus, cutting away the lower third of the stalk,
and place in the boiling water. Cook for 15–20 minutes until tender. Remove, and
douse with cold water.

Arrange the lettuce on a plate. Wrap each piece of asparagus in a piece of ham
so that the tip is still visible. Place on top of the lettuce. Chop the tomato and egg
into small cubes. Together with the zucchini cubes, sprinkle over the asparagus.
Garnish with chervil and drops of walnut oil.

**SIMMERING TIME:** Asparagus according to size, 15–20 minutes

# SACHER ROLLS WITH MUSHROOM AND TAFELSPITZ SPREAD

**INGREDIENTS for 20 rolls**

20 baguette-like rolls · 250 g Tafelspitz
(boiled round of beef, smoked), Bresaola,
dry-salted beef or prosciutto · 100 g mushrooms
40 ml olive oil · 125 g curd cheese (with 20 % fat)
125 g Gervais (cream cheese) · 1 Tbsp chopped
chives · pinch of ground caraway seeds · salt
pepper · 1 sprig each of thyme and rosemary

**PREPARATION**

Slice mushrooms finely and sauté in hot oil with thyme,
rosemary, salt, pepper until all liquid has evaporated.
Remove herbs and let the mushrooms cool. Dice the
smoked meat.

Purée all the ingredients in a blender, and season to taste.
Slice the rolls lengthways leaving the halves connected
and open enough to apply the spread. Put the mixture in
a pastry bag with a smooth nozzle and squeeze into the
opening. Add optional garnish.

# FIAKER GOULASH
# WITH SACHER SAUSAGES

**INGREDIENTS for 4–6 servings**

1 kg shank of beef (or any type of stewing beef) · 4–6 eggs
4–6 pickled gherkins · 2–3 pairs of Sacher sausages (or Frankfurter
or Wieners) · 750 g onions · 150 g dripping or oil · 2 Tbsps of
sweet paprika powder · 1 tsp Rosen paprika powder or spicy
paprika powder · 3 cloves of garlic · 1 Tbsp puréed tomatoes
(or 1–2 cooking spoons of tomato paste) · 1 Tbsp marjoram
2 bay leaves · 1 tsp chopped caraway seeds · vinegar · salt
ground pepper · butter for frying eggs

Cut the onions in strips, the meat in cubes, and crush the garlic. Heat the dripping or oil in a pot and fry onions on medium heat until golden brown. Add the paprika powder and tomato paste, stir, and quickly pour in the vinegar and a little water. Mix the cubed meat with salt and pepper, and add to the pot.

Stir in the garlic, marjoram, bay leaves and caraway, and pour in enough water so that the meat is covered. Stir, and simmer on medium heat, semi-covered, for about 2 1/2 hours. Stir from time to time, and add water. As soon as the meat is cooked, take the pot off the stove and place in a moderately-warm oven for about 1 hour.

Meanwhile, heat water for the sausages. Simmer for about 10 minutes.

Heat the butter in a pan, and fry the eggs. Slice the gherkins in the shape of a fan.

Heat the goulash again, add water if needed, season, and stir vigorously.

When the goulash is ready, serve on warmed plates. Place the fried eggs on top of the goulash, and one sausage on the side. Garnish with gherkins.

**COOKING TIME:**
Depending on the meat, 2 1/2–3 hours

**SUGGESTED SIDE DISHES:**
Bread dumplings, boiled potatoes, red pepper salad

*Sacher*

# CLASSIC
# STARTERS

*Sacher*        CLASSIC STARTERS

# SACHER TAFELSPITZ ASPIC WITH LAMB'S LETTUCE

INGREDIENTS for 1 triangular, tureen-shaped
baking tray with 1.3 l volume

**600 g boiled round of beef (Tafelspitz) (see p. 105) · 6 cl dry sherry
2 carrots · 2 yellow turnips · 1/4 celeriac · 4 Tbsps chopped chives
600 ml beef stock · 10 sheets of gelatin
Oil for greasing · ground pepper · salt · 200 g field salad
Pumpkin seed pesto (or traditional pesto) · chives for decoration**

FOR THE MARINADE

**4 Tbsps corn oil · 3 Tbsps apple vinegar · 2 Tbsps beef stock
pinch of salt**

PREPARATION

Boil the stock in 200 ml water. Add the carrots, turnip and celeriac and cook until soft. Remove from the soup and allow to cool, then cut into strips about 3 mm thick. Soak the gelatin in cold water, drain and add to the soup. Season the soup with sherry, salt and pepper. Remove from heat.

Grease the tray with oil. Line the base with plastic wrap, smoothing it out with kitchen paper.

Cut the boiled beef into slices about 2 mm thick (bread-cutting machine recommended). Dip each slice into the warm soup and line the tray with the meat, letting it hang about 6 cm over the edge of the tray. Add a little soup, and sprinkle chives over the meat. Place the vegetable strips lengthways over the meat and place more meat on top. Repeat three times. Pour in the rest of the soup, and fold in the overlapping pieces of meat. Cover with plastic wrap, pressing it down over the mass, and refrigerate for 3 hours.

Mix all the marinade ingredients with a whisk and use it to marinate the salad.

Once the aspic is set, turn it upside down on a tray, and remove the plastic wrap. Cut the aspic into slices.

Serve on cooled plates and decorate with the marinated salad. Dribble a few drops of pesto over the aspic, and sprinkle with chives.

## GERMAN HARDNESS

*The German Federal Chancellor Konrad Adenauer often enjoyed the Sacher Hotel's cuisine on his numerous visits to Vienna, especially the "Tafelspitz".*
*"Why isn't it possible to serve such a tender piece of meat in Bonn?" he asked once, almost annoyed.*
*The head waiter, not one to forgo a comment, answered dryly: "Perhaps, Mr. Chancellor, it has something to do with the fact that we Austrians have simply always been the softer ones. That's why we already have our treaty, and the hard Germans still don't have one!"*

39

# ORIGINAL SACHER GOOSE-LIVER CAKE

INGREDIENTS for 1 cake with a 22 cm Ø

### GOOSE-LIVER CAKE
350 g Goose-liver terrine from a delicatessen, room temperature
200 ml cream, room temperature · 4 sheets of gelatin · 2 cl Port wine · salt

### FOR THE APRICOT CHUTNEY
250 g pitted dried apricots · 2 cl white balsamic vinegar · 1 small shallot
1 cooking spoon sugar · grated ginger · lemongrass, finely cut
fresh chilies, finely cut · salt

### FOR THE APRICOT FILLING
100 g pitted dried apricots · 1 cooking spoon sugar
1 Tbsp white balsamic vinegar · 1 Tbsp Périgord truffle cubes

### FOR THE ICE WINE JELLY
50 ml consommé or strong beef stock · 2 sheets gelatin · 50 ml ice wine
(wine made from grapes hardened by frost)

### FOR COMPLETION
200 g goose-liver terrine · 100 g melted bitter couverture
(with at least 70 % cocoa content) · 2 cl old apple brandy or Calvados
1 layer of original Sacher Torte for the base, 5 mm high and 22 cm Ø

(see Sacher Torte recipe)

For the mousse, soak gelatin in cold water, drain. Melt into the port wine at about 60 °C. Beat the cream until semi-stiff. Mix together the room-temperature terrine and port wine-gelatin mixture and put through a fine sieve. Fold in the salt and cream.

For the chutney, rinse jam jars with hot water. Cook all the ingredients in approx. 400 ml water for 10 minutes. Mix the chutney well, and then strain. Pour into the jars, and set aside to cool. (The chutney can be stored for about a month and is an excellent condiment for meat and game dishes).

For the apricot filling, cut the dried apricots into fine cubes, and simmer in 250 ml of water with the sugar and vinegar. Add the truffle cubes, and allow to cool.

For the ice wine jelly, soak the gelatin in cold water, drain, and pour in some of the hot soup. Allow to dissolve, then mix with the rest of the soup and the ice wine.

For the final stage, take a flat baking tray and cover it with plastic wrap. In the approximate shape of the cake, spread the melted chocolate thinly onto the plastic. Place the layer of the Sacher Torte on top of the chocolate and put the cake form around the base. Sprinkle the cake layer with a few drops of apple brandy and spread on the mousse about 1 cm thick. Cut the goose-liver terrine into slices about 5–6 mm thick and place across the mousse. Spread the mousse (about 5 mm thick) over the terrine and then apply the apricot filling thinly over the middle area of the cake. Smooth on the remaining mousse and allow to cool for one hour. Cover with the ice wine jelly, and refrigerate for 1 hour. Carefully remove the cake ring and cut into 12 equal pieces.

Serve with brioches (see Breakfast) or hippen (a type of thin wafer).

# THE WAITER WHO DIDN'T DROP TO THE GROUND

*Shah Reza Pahlevi of Persia, who often spent time in Vienna, always gave a reception for the Persian embassy on his visits. The diplomats waited in the hall, and the Shah would enter later. He was received by Herbert Müller, head of the banquet, and greeted with a "Je vous en pris", and then led to his compatriots. As was custom as the Shah entered, those present dropped to the floor, and Müller led the Shah to his chair.*

*"Who dares not bow before the Shah?" one of the diplomats hissed.*

*"That's the head waiter from the Hotel Sacher," another answered in a whisper.*

Sacher

# SACHER'S FINEST SOUPS AND SOUP GARNISHES

# CLASSIC VIENNESE BEEF SOUP

**INGREDIENTS for 6 servings**

**500 g beef for boiling (first-cut flank, brisket or chuck) · bones**
**herbs and vegetables for making soup**
**1/2 onion · 3 egg whites · salt · some chives or parsley**

**PREPARATION**

Wash the meat and pat dry with kitchen paper. Cut into cubes and place in 2 liters of cold water. Fry the onion without fat in an (old) pan on the cut surface until golden brown. Wash the bones in cold water and, together with the soup vegetables and onions, add to the meat. Bring to the boil and let simmer for about 2 hours. Let the soup cool and skim off the fat.
Whisk the egg whites with 250 ml of cold water, and stir slowly into the soup. Simmer until it becomes transparent. Drain through a dish towel, and add salt to taste. Serve as a transparent soup, (with sprinkled chives or parsley) or with the following Viennese soup garnishes.

**SIMMERING TIME:** Approx. 2 hours

## THE ARISTOCRATIC WAITER

*The Hotel Sacher now and then employed people of aristocratic descent. At one time a young pageboy was working there. During an opera ball dinner, one of the guests, who thought he hadn't been served quickly enough, shouted: "Don't you know who I am? I am the Duke of Bavaria!" The head waiter called over the pageboy and, introducing him to the duke, said, "What's the problem? Here, the pageboys are counts."*

# CLASSIC VIENNESE SOUP GARNISHES

## SEMOLINA DUMPLINGS

### INGREDIENTS

**100 g coarse semolina · 40 g butter, room temperature
1 medium-sized egg, separated (approx. 50 g) · salt
ground white pepper · ground nutmeg · butter for greasing
ice cubes**

### PREPARATION

Beat the butter until fluffy. Stir the egg yolk into the butter. Briefly whip the egg white and gradually combine with the butter mixture. Season with salt, pepper and nutmeg. Stir in the semolina, adding more salt, pepper and nutmeg to taste, and refrigerate for about 10 minutes. Form small, ellipse-shaped dumplings using two spoons, dipping them into warm water to clean. Place the dumplings on greaseproof paper smeared with butter and set aside to cool for about 10 minutes. Heat water in a pot and add salt. Slide the dumplings in, and bring water to boil once. Add some ice to the water. Take the pot off the stove, put a piece of grease-proof paper smeared with butter on top of the water, cover the pot and let sit for about 20 minutes. Remove the dumplings, and serve in the soup.

**COOKING TIME:** Briefly boil; let stand for 20 minutes

## FRITTATEN (crêpe slivers)

### INGREDIENTS for 6 servings

**75 g flour, fine · 125 ml milk · 2 eggs · salt · 30 g butter**

### PREPARATION

Prepare a crêpe mix with the flour, milk, eggs and salt. Heat the butter in a pan and make thin crêpes from the mixture, frying them a golden brown on both sides. Roll up each crêpe individually and slice finely. Distribute the slivers in a soup bowl, and pour over hot soup.

# FRITTATEN SOUP AND VALKYRIES

*"A genius in his field"* is how Sacher Hotel head waiter Wolfgang Ebner fondly remembers opera expert Prof. Marcel Prawy. *"But life outside the opera actually didn't interest him at all."*

His favorite dish was "Frittaten soup à la Prawy", which contained more frittaten (slivers of crêpe) than it did soup. However Professor "Marcello" was even oblivious to his favorite dish.

One night, as he often did, Prawy was sitting at the table with his music colleagues, debating about Wagner's 'Valkyries', the themes from which he loudly sang. Suddenly, whilst riding on the Valkyrie melody, he stopped and asked: *"Mr. Ebner, have I actually eaten today?"*

*"Yes, Professor,"* the waiter answered.

*"And did I like it?"*

*"Judging by your expression, you were satisfied."*

*"Well, everything's okay then,"* said Prawy.

And on rode the Valkyries.

## VEAL LIVER DUMPLINGS

### INGREDIENTS

**120 g veal liver · 2 pieces of chicken liver · 40 g bread crumbs
1 slice of toast, without crust · 50 ml milk · 1 egg · 1 small shallot
1 clove of garlic, finely chopped · 3 Tbsps of pork lard · salt
parsley, chopped · ground pepper · marjoram, finely chopped**

### PREPARATION

Finely chop the shallot and sauté in hot lard, then let stand.

Soak the toast in slightly warmed milk. Drain the toast well and then mince it with the veal and chicken liver, and shallots. Mix in the breadcrumbs and egg, and season with garlic, salt, parsley, pepper and marjoram. Cover, and leave to stand in a cool place for about 20–30 minutes.

Bring to boil a large pot of salt water. With moist hands, form dumplings from the mixture. Place dumplings in the water and simmer for 8–10 minutes. Remove with a draining spoon, and serve in hot beef soup.

### SIMMERING TIME: 8–10 minutes

*Sacher*

SOUPS AND SOUP GARNISHES

# VIENNESE POTATO SOUP

## INGREDIENTS for 4–6 servings

**1.5 l beef stock · 300 g potatoes · 100 g fresh mushrooms (porcini, chanterelle etc.) · 50 g bacon · 50 g onion, chopped · 120 g root vegetables (carrots, turnips, parsnips) · 4 Tbsps butter · 1 Tbsp flour · 125 ml cream 1 bay leaf · marjoram · caraway seeds, ground · 1–2 cloves of garlic, crushed · ground pepper · salt · dash of white wine · chives**

## PREPARATION

Cut the potatoes and vegetables into 1 cm cubes and divide in the ratio 1:2. Clean the mushrooms with a moist cloth or sponge. Separate the caps from the stems and cut into bite-size pieces. In a casserole dish, heat the butter and sauté the chopped onions. Add about a third of the vegetables and the potatoes, as well as the mushroom stems, and sauté. Dust with some flour and add a dash of white wine. Pour in about 1 1/4 liters of beef stock and stir. Bring to the boil, and season with marjoram, bay leaf, caraway seeds, garlic, freshly ground pepper and salt.

Simmer for about 10 minutes then take out the bay leaf. Purée the soup, and strain. Add the rest of the vegetables and potatoes to the remaining beef stock and steam for about 10–15 minutes or until they are soft.

In a pan, fry the chopped bacon and mushroom caps. To the soup, now add the mushrooms, steamed vegetables and potatoes. Stir in the cream and bring to boil briefly. Add salt and pepper to taste.

Serve in warmed soup bowls, and sprinkle over some chopped chives.

**SIMMERING TIME:** Approx. 15–20 minutes

## POTATO SOUP "AL HARAM"

*Jaroslav Müller, the long-time master of Sacher cuisine, speaks many languages, including Arabic.*

*When a Jordanian royal once ordered the potato soup, Müller used the phrase "al haram", referring to the fact that it is a sin for Muslims to eat it because the croutons are tossed in bacon fat. His Excellency smiled, and pretended not to hear the chef, whereupon Müller served him the 'sinful soup' exactly as it was meant to be served: complete with bacon.*

# OLD-STYLE VIENNESE CHICKEN SOUP

INGREDIENTS for 6–8 servings
1 chicken, approx. 1.8 kg, ready to cook · root vegetables (parsley,
carrots, celery stalk) for soup · 1 onion · 4 peppercorns
3 allspice corns · 1 bay leaf · 2 cloves · 1 small sprig thyme · 40 g butter
40 g flour · 100 g mushrooms · 150 g cooked peas · 1 egg yolk
150 ml cream · salt · pepper · butter for sautéing
1 Tbsp finely chopped chives · croutons, fried

## PREPARATION

Wash and clean the chicken. Place the chicken and the innards, except the liver,
in 2–3 liters of cold water and bring to the boil. Add root vegetables. Halve the
onion and fry without fat, cut surface down, at maximum heat in a preferably old
pan until almost black.

Put the herbs in a linen bag, tie it, and place in the soup with the onions.

Skim foam and fat as they come to the surface. During the last 10 minutes, add the
chicken liver to the soup. As soon as the meat is tender, put the soup through a
sieve. Remove the chicken meat from the bones and cut into small pieces, along
with the innards.

Heat some butter in a large pot, mix in the flour, and pour in the chicken soup,
letting it cook for at least another 30 minutes.

Slice the mushrooms finely and sauté in butter. Purée the peas. Add the
mushrooms to the soup and let simmer. Combine the puréed peas and the cream.
Stir into the soup and cook until creamy. Add the chicken to the soup, and briefly
cook.

Remove the soup from the stove and mix in the beaten egg yolk. Add salt and
pepper to taste. Serve with croutons and a sprinkling of chopped chives.

SIMMERING TIME: Chicken, approx. 1 hour; soup 40–50 minutes

Sacher

# FINE INTERIM COURSES

# OLD-STYLE VIENNESE SALON BEUSCHEL WITH BREAD DUMPLINGS

**INGREDIENTS for Beuschel**
**(ragout made with heart and lungs)**

**600 g veal lungs · 1 veal heart · 1 root vegetables (parsley, carrots, celery stalk) · 6 peppercorns · 3 allspice corns · 1 bay leaf 1 small sprig thyme · 1 small onion · salt**

**FINAL STAGE**

**40 g butter · 30 g flour · 1 cooking spoon capers · 1 small onion, halved 1 anchovy fillet, finely chopped · 1 clove garlic, chopped · lemon rind, grated · 1 Tbsp parsley, finely chopped · dash of vinegar · sugar pinch of ground marjoram · smidgen of mustard · 2 Tbsps sour cream 2 Tbsps cream · dash of lemon juice · salt · ground pepper 4 Tbsps goulash sauce for serving**

**INGREDIENTS for 6 medium-sized bread dumplings**

**200 g bread cubes · 3 eggs · approx. 180 ml milk, hot · 2 shallots, finely chopped · 50 g butter · salt · nutmeg, grated · 2 Tbsp parsley, chopped · 1 Tbsps cornstarch (Maizena) · 100 g flour, coarse**

**PREPARATION OF THE INNARDS**

Separate the veal lung from the windpipe and gullet. Soak well, piercing several holes in the lung so that water can get into the cavity.

Fry the onion, cut surfaces down, in a pan until golden brown. Fill a large pot with cold water, add lungs and heart and bring to boil. Add to the pot the root vegetables, peppercorns, allspice corns, bay leaf, thyme, salt and onion. Simmer until meat is tender.

Remove the lung after about 1 hour and rinse with cold water to cool. Leave the heart in the stock for at least another 30 minutes, until very tender, then remove.

Heat some of the stock in another saucepan and bring to boil. Meanwhile, cut the lung and heart finely, removing any cartilage.

For the final stage, heat some butter in a casserole dish. Sprinkle in the flour and sauté until light brown. Add the finely chopped 'innards seasoning': capers, onion, anchovy fillet, garlic, lemon rind, and parsley. Let draw on low heat for a few minutes. Add the reduced stock, stir well and cook for 15–20 minutes until thick. Add the innards and season with salt, pepper, vinegar, sugar, marjoram and mustard. As soon as the ragout is thick, stir in the sour cream and cream. Simmer for another 5–10 minutes. Add lemon juice to taste and serve with a few drops of hot goulash juice.

## BREAD DUMPLINGS

Sauté the shallots in butter until golden brown, then toss the bread cubes in the butter. Place the contents of the pan into a large bowl and add the eggs, milk, cornstarch, salt, nutmeg, and parsley. Mix all the ingredients together well. Add bread cubes if needed.

Let stand for about 15 minutes. Form round dumplings from the mass with moist hands. Dip lightly into the flour, and shape.

Boil some salt water, put the dumplings in, and simmer for about 15 minutes, shaking the pot from time to time so the dumplings don't stick. Remove, and leave to drain.

**SIMMERING TIME:** Approx. 1 1/2 hours

# ADVICE FROM A FORMER MAITRE 'D

*"The more impossible and disagreeable a guest is, the more politely you put him down. Then you'll have him eating out of your hand."*

# VIENNESE GOULASH

INGREDIENTS for 6–8 servings

1.5 kg beef shank · 1.25 kg onions · 150 g dripping or oil
2 Tbsps tomato paste · 4 Tbsps paprika powder, sweet
2 cloves of garlic · a little lemon rind, grated · apple vinegar
2 juniper berries, pressed · pinch of marjoram
pinch of ground caraway seeds · pinch of sugar · ground pepper
salt · 2 Tbsps flour · approx. 2 l water

PREPARATION

Slice onions. Cut the meat into cubes, approx. 50 g each. Heat the dripping in a large pot and fry the onions until golden brown. Add juniper berries, marjoram, caraway seeds, sugar, pepper and salt and briefly sauté. Stir in paprika powder, tomato paste, garlic and lemon rind and quickly add vinegar and 1 liter of water. Bring to boil then add the cubed meat and let stew for about 2 1/2 hours. Stir repeatedly and add water if necessary.

When the meat is almost done, stir well and add the rest of the water. Let cook for a while longer then add salt to taste. Mix the flour with a bit of water, stir and add to the goulash to bind.

COOKING TIME: Depending on the meat, 2 1/2–3 hours
SUGGESTED SIDE DISHES: Fresh bread rolls or salt potatoes

# CREAMY VIENNESE
# VEAL GOULASH WITH DUMPLINGS

## INGREDIENTS for the goulash

1 kg veal shoulder · 200 g onions · 1 tsp paprika powder, sweet
1 Tbsp Rosen paprika powder · 1 Tbsp tomato paste · 1 apple, sour
250 ml cream · 125 ml sour cream · 20 g flour
juice from one lemon · grated lemon rind · 125 ml white wine
1 bay leaf · salt · ground pepper · 4 Tbsps oil for frying

## INGREDIENTS for the dumplings

250 g flour, fine · 2 eggs · 1 egg yolk · approx. 150 ml milk
1 Tbsp butter, melted · salt · ground nutmeg · butter for frying

## PREPARATION OF THE GOULASH

Cut the meat into bite-size cubes and chop the onions. Heat the oil in a casserole dish and lightly fry the meat. Remove, then sauté the onions. Add the tomato paste and paprika powder and pour on the wine. Add the meat and add water so the meat is just covered. Add the bay leaf, salt and pepper and stew for about 1 1/2 hours.

As soon as the meat is tender, remove again with a draining spoon. Remove the bay leaf. Cut the apple into small cubes and add to the goulash, along with the lemon juice and grated lemon rind. Mix in the flour, cream and sour cream. Stir well.

Bring to boil then mix with a hand-held mixer. Strain the liquid and add the meat again, adding salt and pepper to taste.

## PREPARATION FOR THE DUMPLINGS

In a bowl mix the eggs with the egg yolk and milk. Add flour and melted butter. Season with salt and nutmeg, and mix until smooth. If necessary, add milk or flour. Boil some salt water in a large, wide saucepan and place the dumplings with a dumpling sieve directly into the boiling water. Boil, then strain. Rinse in cold water, drain and sauté in the butter.

**SIMMERING TIME:** 1 1/2 hours

# SZEGEDINER GOULASH

### INGREDIENTS
for 4–6 servings

**600 g pork shoulder**
**500 g sauerkraut · 100 g pork**
**dripping · 150 g onions**
**1 tsp tomato paste · 1 cooking**
**spoon paprika powder, sweet**
**1 tsp Rosen paprika powder**
**2 bay leaves · 2 cloves of garlic,**
**chopped · caraway seeds**
**125 ml heavy cream**
**125 ml sour cream · 1/2 Tbsp**
**flour · salt · ground pepper**
**beef stock or water**

### PREPARATION

Cut the meat into bite-size cubes and chop the onions. Heat the oil in a casserole dish and lightly fry the meat. Remove, then sauté the onions until golden yellow. Add the tomato paste and both paprika powders and pour on some water. Add the meat again, and stir in the bay leaf, garlic, caraway seeds, salt and pepper. Pour in some beef stock or water and stew for about 1 1/2 hours. After about 40 minutes, while the meat is stewing, add sauerkraut and if necessary, add water or stock. (There should never be too much fluid, but just enough to cover the meat).

As soon as the meat and sauerkraut are tender, combine the cream, sour cream and flour and stir until smooth. Add to the stew and stir well. Cook for another 10 minutes on medium heat, until the goulash is thick. Serve on warmed plates.

**COOKING TIME:** Approx. 1 1/2 hours
**SUGGESTED SIDE DISHES:** Salt potatoes

**TIP:** Served with a dollop of sour cream, the goulash looks even better

# SACHER-STYLE REISFLEISCH
## (Meat with Rice)

INGREDIENTS for 6 servings

1 kg veal or beef cheek (alternatively, beef shoulder) · 300 g risotto rice
2–2.5 liters beef stock or vegetable stock · 500 g onions, cut in fine rings
1 bulb of garlic, cut in half with skin · 200 ml red wine · 1 Tbsp paprika powder
1 cooking spoon sugar · 300 g canned tomatoes, peeled · 1 bay leaf
1 small sprig marjoram · caraway seeds, whole · 4 Tbsp parmesan
1 red and 1 green pepper · salt · ground pepper · flour · pork dripping
or olive oil for sautéeing · butter for the risotto · marjoram or thyme
for decoration

*Sacher*

FINE INTERIM COURSES

## PREPARATION

Clean the meat and chop into bite-size pieces and season with pepper and salt. Dredge in flour. Using an ovenproof pan, quickly fry the meat in dripping or olive oil. Remove from the pan. Sauté the onion rings in the pan until transparent, then add the bay leaf, caraway seeds, sugar and marjoram. Add the meat again, and place in a preheated oven (at 180 °C) and braise for about 40 minutes. Spoon out about 300 ml of the meat juice and strain it to use for the risotto.

After about 40 minutes, stir into the pan the paprika powder, and quickly pour in the red wine and some stock. Add the garlic and tomatoes and cook for another 60–80 minutes, regularly turning the meat over in the juices and adding stock if necessary.

About 20 minutes before the meat is done, sauté the risotto rice in butter and pour over about 300 ml of the cooking liquid. Add about 150 ml more stock, bring to the boil and, stirring regularly, cook for about 18 minutes until the rice is al dente. If necessary add more stock so that the risotto becomes nice and creamy. Bind with parmesan and piece of cold butter about the size of a nut.

While the risotto is binding, seed the peppers and cut into thick strips. Cook in olive oil until tender.

Test the meat with a knife to see if it's tender. If so, remove it and keep warm. If the sauce has become too thick, thin it with some stock. Strain the sauce through a strainer, and season to taste.

Serve the meat with the rice on warmed, deep plates. Briefly sauté the peppers in olive oil and place on the plates. Decorate with marjoram or thyme and pour over the sauce.

**COOKING TIME:** 100–120 minutes; risotto approx. 20 minutes
**OVEN TEMPERATURE:** 180 °C

# SCHINKENFLECKERL ("Ham Pasta") COVERED WITH BAKED CHEESE

## INGREDIENTS

**200–250 g ham (recommended: Prager ham) or cooked smoked pork**
**3 egg yolks · 2 eggs · 3 egg whites · 80 g butter, room temperature**
**250 ml sour cream · 150 ml cream · salt · ground pepper · ground nutmeg**
**bread crumbs and grated parmesan · butter for the baking tray**

## FOR THE NOODLES

**(or use approx. 200 g ready-made square, flat noodles)**
**approx. 250 g flour, coarse · 1 egg · 2 egg yolks · salt · water**
**flour for the work surface**

## PREPARATION

Either boil the ready-made pasta, or make it fresh.

To make it fresh, make smooth, elastic pasta dough using the flour, egg, egg yolks, salt and water. On a working surface dusted with flour, roll out the dough thinly with a rolling pin and cut into small squares. Leave to dry. Bring a large saucepan of water to boil and cook the pasta until al dente, 3–5 minutes. Drain, rinse with cold water and drain again.

In a bowl, beat together the butter, eggs, egg yolk, and a pinch of salt until the mixture is fluffy. Dice the ham and add to the egg mixture. Whisk the egg white with a pinch of salt and then fold into the egg mixture together with the sour cream, cream and pasta.

Mix thoroughly, and season with pepper, salt and nutmeg. Place the noodle-ham mixture into a deep baking tray greased with butter, and sprinkle over the breadcrumbs and freshly grated parmesan. Place a few flakes of butter on top to melt while cooking.

Preheat the oven to 180 °C and bake for about 45 minutes. Remove, and serve on warmed plates.

**BAKING TIME:** Approx. 45 minutes
**BAKING TEMPERATURE:** 180 °C
**SUGGESTED SIDE DISHES:** Lettuce salad

# STUFFED PEPPERS, SACHER-STYLE

## INGREDIENTS

**4 red peppers · 300 g potatoes · 4 small shallots, peeled and chopped
300 g Braunschweiger sausage, cubed · 3 Tbsps cheese, grated
100 g sour cream · 1 egg · 1 cooking spoon fresh marjoram, finely
chopped · 2 Tbsp parsley, chopped · 1 Tbsp capers, finely chopped
Tabasco sauce · 6 very ripe tomatoes · 2 Tbsps sugar · 2 fresh bay leaves
5 Tbsps olive oil for frying · 2 Tbsps pork dripping, melted,
or vegetable oil · salt · ground pepper · caraway seeds (whole)
ground nutmeg**

## PREPARATION

Wash the peppers and cut off the caps. Remove the seeds and white flesh. Also
remove these from the caps of the peppers, and fashion a round lid.

Cut the potatoes in 4 mm cubes and sauté with shallots in the olive oil. Season with
salt, pepper, caraway seeds and nutmeg and add about 300 ml water. Steam
for about 10 minutes. As soon as the water has evaporated, add the sausage.
Stir well.

Stir in the sour cream, marjoram, parsley, capers, egg and cheese, and season
with pepper and salt. Fill the peppers with the mixture, push down well, and place
the lids on top.

Brush the peppers with dripping or oil and place on an ovenproof pan or dish.
Mash together the tomatoes, sugar, bay leaves, salt, and a shot of Tabasco and add
to the dish. Preheat the fan-forced oven at 180 °C and bake for 40–50 minutes.

While the peppers are baking, stir the sauce repeatedly. When the peppers are
tender, remove from the oven and place on a warmed plate. Purée the sauce
and let simmer for a little longer if necessary. Pour over the stuffed peppers.

**COOKING TIME:** 40–50 minutes
**OVEN TEMPERATURE:** 180 °C in a fan-forced oven
**SUGGESTED SIDE DISHES:** Lettuce salad

## WANNINGER'S OPERA BALL TRICK

*Peter Wanninger worked in the Sacher Hotel reception for 45 years (1958–2003). His first 30 years were as head porter, and the last 15, as supervisor of eight porters and 14 pageboys.*

*Wanninger, upon whom the porter was based in the TV series "Hello, Hotel Sacher, Portier", was a rather slim figure in contrast with Fritz Eckhardt, the actor who played Wanninger's character.*

*Amongst his colleagues, Wanninger was famous for his "Wanninger Trick", which he used on New Year's Eve and for the Opera ball: His working day would begin at a quarter past five in the morning, and would end only when the last guests left the Sacher for the Opera ball late in the evening. He would then go to bed, get up before dawn the next morning, and be standing washed, combed, and dressed to the nines, in his porter's box.*

*"The guests were really impressed," recalls Wanninger, "because they actually thought I'd spent the whole night awake because of them."*

## ONION QUICHE "SACHER ECK"

INGREDIENTS for 1 spring form or tart form, 28 cm Ø
**300 g flour · 150 g butter · 80 g curd cheese (20 % fat), drained
2 egg yolks · pinch of salt · flour for the work surface · 500 g white onion
approx. 150 g lean bacon, finely cut · 1 bunch spring onions · 1/2 leek
8 Tbsps olive oil**

### FOR THE FILLING
**5 eggs · 250 ml cream · 80 g Gouda cheese or other mild cheese, grated
salt · ground pepper · nutmeg · butter for greasing**

### PREPARATION
For the pastry, mix flour, butter, cottage cheese, egg yolks and a pinch of salt.
Quickly knead until smooth. Wrap in plastic and refrigerate for 4 hours.

Halve the onions, and slice. Heat the olive oil in a pan. Sauté the onions (without the spring onions), stirring them quickly until they are transparent. Remove from heat and allow to cool.

Preheat the oven to 200 °C. Grease the cake form with butter. On top of a floured surface, roll out the dough with a rolling pin about 3mm thick and place in the tray so that about 2 cm of it hangs over the edge. Distribute the onions equally over the dough.

For the filling, whisk the eggs and the cream. Cut the leek and spring onions (only the white part) into rings and mix into the egg mixture with the bacon and cheese. Pour over the pastry. To form an attractive crust, use thumb and forefinger to shape the edge of the pastry around the edges of the tart form.

Bake for about 40 minutes. Remove from the oven and leave to sit for about 10 minutes before cutting.

**BAKING TIME:** Approx. 40 minutes
**OVEN TEMPERATURE:** 200 °C

# THE TENOR'S WOMEN

*"La donna è mobile", is what the Count from Mantua sings in Verdi's "Rigoletto", and tenors seem to have a particularly easy game with the hearts of women. And their wives know it, too.*

*Along with the porters, the chamber maids and pageboys of Hotel Sacher, the "tenor's wife" is something of a figurine in hotel life. If she's not sitting in a theater box during the performance, she sits nervously by the porter's office in great anticipation of her husband, who has god-like status. Based on numerous examples, above all the wives of Franco Corelli und Mario del Monaco, many of those in the know will say that the tenor's wife is known for being one thing: jealous.*

# "TROUT QUARTET" WITH FRESHWATER TROUT, NOODLES, SPINACH AND TROUT CAVIAR

## INGREDIENTS

**8 small trout fillets, 40–50 g each, de-boned, but with skin**
**2 handfuls of young fresh spinach · 4 Tbsps trout or arctic char caviar**
**2 Tbsps butter or brown butter · salt · white ground pepper**
**2 Tbsps olive oil · parsley for decoration**

## FOR THE SAUCE

**100 ml dry white wine· 2 cl Noilly-Prat · 300 ml fish stock · 1 cooking spoon horseradish, freshly chopped or grated · 2 Tbsps butter, cold · salt**

## FOR THE PASTA DOUGH

**160 g flour · 80 g coarse semolina · 1 egg · 2 egg yolks**
**flour for the work surface · egg for brushing · salt**

## PREPARATION

For the pasta dough, combine the flour, semolina, egg, egg yolks, a pinch of salt and some water. Knead into a firm dough. Wrap in plastic and leave to sit for at least an hour in a cool place. Using a rolling pin, roll out the dough thinly on a floured surface, and cut into squares (approx. 8 x 8 cm). Take one corner and roll crossways (see photo) to the other corner. Brush the connecting point with the egg and press together so it holds.

For the sauce, heat the Noilly-Prat and about a third of the white wine and simmer until it reduces to about a third. Pour on the fish juice and again simmer until the liquid reduces to about 150 ml. Stir in the horseradish and bind with the cold butter. Add salt to taste.

Season the de-boned fish fillets with salt and pepper and place them skin side down on an ovenproof plate brushed with oil. Cover with aluminum foil and bake in the preheated oven (85 °C) for about 15–20 minutes. While the fish is cooking, cook the noodles al dente, but don't douse with cold water. Heat butter in a pan and toss the spinach until it softens. Add the noodles the pan, and salt to taste.

Arrange decoratively on a plate, with the fish, either with or without skin. Dribble over the sauce, and serve with caviar. Decorate with parsley.

**COOKING TIME:** Trout, 15–20 minutes; a few minutes for the noodles
**OVEN TEMPERATURE:** 85 °C

# SACHER À LA VÉGÉTARIENNE

# FRIED WATERMELON WITH SMOKED SHEEP'S CHEESE

### INGREDIENTS

**500 g watermelon (ripe), without seeds · juice from 1/2 a lime · fresh mint lemon balm leaves · 300 g smoked sheep's cheese · optional red chili (without seeds), finely chopped · sea salt · ground pepper · olive oil Kalamata olives and crisply fried bread chips for optional decoration**

### PREPARATION

Cut the watermelon in 12 equally long pieces (approx. 12 x 2 x 2 cm). Before frying, pat with a kitchen paper. Fry briefly in a teflon-lined pan with some olive oil. Place 3 pieces each on a warm plate.

Slice the cheese very thinly with a grater and place over the melon. Sprinkle with the herbs, some olive oil, lime juice, and season with salt, pepper and chili. Decorate with olives and pan-fried bread chips.

# BOHEMIAN MUSHROOM GOULASH

INGREDIENTS for 4–6 servings

**400 g mushrooms of choice · 100 g carrots and 100 g celeriac
300 g floury potatoes · 1 bunch spring onions · 60 g butter
150 g shallots · 1 Tbsp paprika powder · 1 bay leaf · 5 juniper berries
pinch of ground caraway seeds · 150 ml white wine· 750 ml chicken stock
150 g sour cream · 1 bunch of dill · 1 sprig lovage · 2–3 Tbsps Most
vinegar (or balsamico) · white ground pepper · salt**

## PREPARATION

Clean mushrooms with a moist sponge (if possible, don't wash). Cut into bite-size pieces. Cut carrots, celeriac, peeled potatoes and spring onions into small cubes. Chop shallots finely.

Heat butter in a pot and sauté the shallots. Add paprika powder, pour over white wine and add all the vegetables (without the mushrooms) as well as the potatoes. Pour in the stock, add salt, pepper and the bay leaf. Boil for 10–15 minutes on high until the broth is thick.

Add mushrooms and simmer for another 5 minutes. Remove the bay leaf, and juniper berries.

Mix the sour cream with some hot stock or water. Add the dill and lovage to the goulash. Let simmer for a few more minutes, then add vinegar to taste.

**COOKING TIME:** Approx. 15–20 minutes
**SUGGESTED SIDE DISHES:** Garlic bread made with rye bread

# ASPARAGUS WATER/VODKA COCKTAIL

*After hunting trips with Leopold Figl, Russian Foreign Minister Vjaceslav Molotov and Foreign Trade Minister Anastas Mikojan were often the Austrian Chancellor's guests in the Sacher hunting salon. Following Figl's motto, "Tell me what's true and drink only clear brew", both Russian guests enjoyed their vodka, and consumed a great deal of it along with even larger amounts of Viennese spring water.*

*One day, recalls head waiter Herbert Müller, asparagus with mousseline sauce was served at the Molotov table with the customary bowl of warm water to cleanse the fingers. What happened next was foreseeable: The Russian guests ate the asparagus, threw down some vodka, and then the finger water – upon which Anastas Mikojan affably said: "Vodka well chilled in Vienna, but water much too warm."*

*Even when he had drunk too much, Mikojan proved to be steadfast. Following another merry banquet, the foreign minister planted himself in front of a crystal mirror, scrutinized his compatriots and said, amazed: "I know we are large delegation, but I not know delegation so big."*

## OVEN ASPARAGUS FROM THE MARCHFELD

### INGREDIENTS

**24 equally sized stalks asparagus · 1 tsp sugar · approx. 150 g butter, slightly burnt · optional 2 Tbsps chopped herbs (chervil, tarragon and parsley) · juice from 2 oranges and some rind, grated · sea salt**

### PREPARATION

Peel asparagus and cut away the lower third of the stalk. Place 6 pieces on two layers of aluminum foil. Sprinkle over some salt and sugar, then melted butter and orange juice, orange rind, chopped herbs (optional). Wrap the asparagus well in the foil.

Place the wrapped packages next to each other on a baking tray and put on the lowest shelf of the oven heated at 220 °C. Bake for 40 minutes.

Take the asparagus out of the oven, leave in the foil for a few minutes. Open the packages at the table in order to enjoy the fine caramel aroma.

COOKING TIME: Approx. 40 minutes
OVEN TEMPERATURE: 220 °C
SUGGESTED SIDE DISHES: Potatoes tossed in parsley, and lettuce salad

# EIERNOCKERLN (Egg Dumplings)

### INGREDIENTS

**300 g flour, fine · 3 eggs for the dumpling mix · 4 eggs for the
egg mixture · approx. 150 ml milk · 2 Tbsps butter, melted
2 Tbsps butter or lard for frying · some oil for the dumplings
salt · pepper · ground nutmeg · chives for decoration**

### PREPARATION

In a large pot, combine flour, melted butter, eggs and a pinch of salt and mix well
with the milk. Mix until the batter becomes smooth and not too thick. Add more
milk if necessary.

Bring salt water to boil in a large pot. Using a spaezle slicer, let the batter drip directly into the boiling water (otherwise the dumplings will stick together). As soon as
the dumplings begin to float at the top of the water, drain them and douse with
cold water. Dribble in a few drops of oil, and stir through so the dumplings
don't stick together.

Toss the dumplings well in a pan with butter.

Season the eggs with salt, pepper and nutmeg and stir. Pour over the dumplings
and cook for no more than two minutes.

Serve the egg dumplings on a warmed plate and sprinkle with chives.

SUGGESTED SIDE DISHES: Lettuce salad                                    71

# PORCINI-POTATO FRITTERS
# WITH LAMB'S LETTUCE

## INGREDIENTS

**4 medium-sized, solid porcini mushrooms (ideally use those with a dark head) · 3 large potatoes · salt · ground white pepper
pinch of grated nutmeg · 1 Tbsp cornstarch (Maizena) · fat (butter or oil) for frying**

## FOR THE SALAD

**150 g field salad· 4 cl pumpkin seed oil · 2 cl apple vinegar · salt**

## FOR THE CHIVE SAUCE

**250 g sour cream · 2 Tbsp chives, finely chopped · salt · ground pepper**

## PREPARATION

Clean the mushrooms and then wipe with a damp cloth (if possible, don't wash). Preferably with a bread-cutting machine, slice thinly (about 1 mm) and season with pepper and salt.

Peel the potatoes and slice finely – approx. 2 mm thick – and then cut them into equal strips (Julienne). Season with pepper and nutmeg. Press well and mix in the cornstarch. Shape into thin, flat cakes and place on a dish towel. Cover half of the potato cakes with mushrooms and place one cake each on top of those with mushrooms. Flatten each of them a little using a dish towel.

Heat fat in a pan and carefully brown each side. Remove, drain on kitchen paper and place on warmed plates. Salt if needed.

For the chive sauce, mix the sour cream, chopped chives, salt and pepper.

For the salad, make a dressing with the pumpkin seed oil, apple vinegar and salt. Decorate the potato cakes with chive sauce and some lettuce, and serve the rest of the salad as a side dish.

# TO GOD, IT'S APPLE JUICE

For years now, many so-called "oil sheikhs" from Saudi Arabia and the United Arab Emirates have remained faithful to Hotel Sacher. Most of them strictly follow the Islamic rule of drinking no alcohol. Yet, in the same way that Osmin discovered his love of grape juice in Mozart's Abduction from the Seraglio, there have been those who have had the same proclivity in Vienna.

In the early Seventies, one of these "black sheep" asked the Sacher waiters to remove the wine labels and replace them with Obi labels (a brand of apple juice). When questioned by a waiter whether it was really necessary, for it was also possible to serve his Excellency wine from a decanter, the sheikh still insisted on the practice.

"Should Allah some day ask me why I defied his alcohol prohibition when I'm standing at the gate of paradise, I can answer 'O lord, it wasn't my fault. I was deceived by the waiters at the Sacher Hotel.'"

73

*Sacher*                                        SACHER À LA VÉGÉTARIENNE

# CLASSIC KRAUTFLECKERL
# (Cabbage-Pasta Bake)

## INGREDIENTS for 6–8 servings

**400 g pasta for fleckerl, small square, flat noodles**
**1 white cabbage head (ideally Spitzkraut) · 100 g vegetable fat**
**(or pork dripping) · 2 onions, chopped · 2 Tbsps sugar · salt**
**caraway seeds · ground pepper**

## PREPARATION

Wash the cabbage and remove the stalk. Cut into quarters, then cut the quarters into smaller pieces. Add salt to taste. Cut the pieces roughly into squares, bruise by hand and let stand for about 15 minutes.

Caramelize the sugar in the fat, and add the cabbage, onions and the caraway seeds. Cover, and cook for about 30 minutes, stirring regularly, until light brown in color. Season with pepper.

Boil some water and cook the noodles until soft, drain and combine with the cabbage. Let stand for a few minutes.

Before serving, season to taste with pepper and salt.

## COOKING TIME:

Noodles approx. 10–12 minutes;
cabbage, approx. 30–40 minutes

# TRUFFLE ALARM

*"Thank goodness it didn't happen very often, but as we had so many high-profile political guests, now and again we had a few bomb scares,"* recalls Jaroslav Müller about one of the darkest moments in his professional life.

*"There was a large gathering, and the waiters were in the process of grating truffles over the plates when it happened. Two minutes later, everyone had vacated, and the only thing left were the untouched plates with two kilos of Alba truffles. The bomb alarm turned out to be a hoax. But the untouched truffles! That was a catastrophe!"*

# POTATO POUCHES WITH TRUFFLES

INGREDIENTS

**500 g floury potatoes· 2 Tbsps cream cheese · 40 g black truffles, preserved · 1 Tbsp truffle oil · 1 egg yolk · 1 Tbsp parmesan, grated salt · veal juice for daubing · egg yolk for daubing flour for the work surface**

**FOR THE PASTA DOUGH**

**200 g flour · 100 g semolina · 1egg · 2 Tbsps water · salt**

**PREPARATION**

To make the dough, combine and knead all the ingredients until smooth. Wrap in plastic and stand in a cool place.

Meanwhile, boil the potatoes in their skins until they are soft. Peel while they are still hot, and put them through a potato ricer. Let the mass cool a little.

Chop the truffles into small cubes, and mix them in with the potato mass along with the cream cheese, truffle oil, egg yolk, parmesan and a pinch of salt.

On a floured surface roll the dough out thinly and, using a cutter or the top of a glass, cut out forms about 8 cm Ø. Place some potato mixture in the middle of each one, brush the edge with egg yolk and fold the rounds in half, pushing the edges to seal.

Boil some salt water, put the pouches in and simmer for about 10 minutes. Remove, and drain. Arrange the pouches on warmed plates and dribble over some veal juice before serving.

**COOKING TIME:** Approx. 10 minutes

**SUGGESTED SIDE DISHES:** Lettuce or tomato salad

# STYRIAN CARP WITH ROOT VEGETABLES AND CARAWAY SEED POTATOES

## INGREDIENTS

1 Mirror carp approx. 1.5–1.8 kg, ready to cook · 500 g small potatoes
salt · pepper corns · 2 bay leaves · 2 juniper berries, lightly crushed
3 cloves of garlic · 10 coriander seeds, roasted · 6 cl apple vinegar
200 ml dry white wine · 2 carrots· 1 turnip · 1 piece of celeriac
1 parsnip · 4 spring onions, whole · 4 Tbsps horseradish, freshly grated
1 small sprig lovage · sea salt · caraway seeds, whole · ground pepper

## PREPARATION

Peel the carrots and turnip, keeping the peel for the stock. Peel the potatoes and boil them in water with caraway seeds until soft.

Wash the carp, pat dry and fillet them from the spine. Cut slits into the skin with a razor blade or sharp knife. Cut the fillets into 2 cm wide strips and set aside. Soak the carcasses (without heads) in water for 1 hour in about 1.5 liters of water. Bring to boil, and while the water is boiling, repeatedly skim off any foam or fat.

Add the herbs, garlic, carrot and turnip peel and simmer for about 20 minutes more then add the vinegar. Drain the stock.

In another saucepan, simmer the wine until the liquid is reduced to 50 ml, and mix with about 500 ml of stock. Slice the peeled vegetables lengthwise with a peeler in very thin strips (or cut very finely). Halve the spring onions, cutting the green very finely.

Place the fillets and vegetables into the spiced stock and simmer for about 5 minutes.

Serve the carp on deep, warmed plates with the potatoes. Sprinkle the fish with horseradish, and garnish with lovage, sea salt and freshly ground pepper.

COOKING TIME: Carp fillets, 5 minutes

# BOHEMIAN CARP IN DARK BEER

## INGREDIENTS

**4 carp fillets, 150–200 g each · 125 ml vinegar · peppercorns
1 bay leaf · 1 small onion· salt**

## FOR THE SAUCE

**125 ml dark beer · 80 g gingerbread crumbs · 60 g almonds, chopped
thinly lengthways · 1 Tbsp nuts, chopped · 1 Tbsp prunes, chopped
2 cooking spoons raisins, soaked in a little beer · 2 Tbsp honey
fish stock · 2 Tbsp butter or lard · optional powidl (type of Austrian
plum jam)**

## PREPARATION

Fill a large pot with about 750 ml of water and add the vinegar, a large pinch of salt, peppercorns, bay leaf and the coarsely chopped onion. Bring to boil, let it boil vigorously for about 5 minutes. Reduce the heat and put the carp fillets in the water. Depending on size, simmer for about 8–10 minutes. Remove, and keep warm. Drain the stock, and set aside.

For the sauce, heat the butter in a pan. On reduced heat, fry the gingerbread crumbs, nuts, almonds, raisins and prunes. Stir in the honey. Spoon in some of the fish stock until the sauce is thick. Pour in the beer and let simmer until the sauce is thick and creamy. Add optional powidl.

Put the carp fillets back in the sauce, turning them over once. Warm them up in the sauce on low heat.

**COOKING TIME:** Approx. 20 minutes

# THE AMUSED QUEEN

*Following an opera performance on one of her official visits to Vienna, Queen Elizabeth II told a master of ceremonies at the Hotel Sacher that she would prefer to sit at a small table-for-eight rather than a long dinner table. She and Prince Philipp along with the Austrian President Franz Jonas, his wife and an interpreter sat down and ordered a bottle of white wine.*

*Head waiter Herbert Müller attended the table personally, served the wine and, as misfortune would have it, tripped over a chair. In order to avoid spilling the wine, he used the queen as a support when he fell. He excused himself by saying, "Excuse me, oh Royal Highness!"*

*The queen reacted regally, and said: "I didn't know that the Austrian waiters were so charming that service begins by kissing my cheeks."*

*On this occasion, the Queen Elizabeth lost a diamond from her tiara. Realizing this later that evening, she asked security to search the opera box she had been occupying. The diamond was eventually found under the Queen's table by an employee of the Sacher Hotel.*

# SERBIAN PIKE-PERCH

## INGREDIENTS
700 g pike-perch fillet · 150 g flour · 4 large potatoes · peanut oil
lemon slices as garnish

## FOR THE PASTE
1 Tbsp paprika powder · 1 Tbsp tomato paste · 1 Tbsp chili paste
1 Tbsp salt · ground pepper · juice from one lemon · 3 cl Worcester sauce
1 clove garlic

## PREPARATION
Using a pestle and mortar, mash all the paste ingredients into a thick paste.

Wash the fillets and pat dry with some kitchen paper. Cut into pieces and, using a razor blade or sharp knife, cut slits about 5 mm deep into the skin. Rub the paste well into the fillets on both sides.

Peel the potatoes and cut into pencil-like strips. Heat the peanut oil (at about 170 °C) and fry the potatoes a golden brown. Remove, and drain on kitchen paper. Keep warm.

Take the fillets and lightly dredge in the flour. Shake off excess flour, and fry for about 5–6 minutes until golden brown. Remove, and drain well. Serve with the potatoes on warmed plates, and garnish with lemon slices.

SUGGESTED SIDE DISHES: Bean salad, pepper salad or a mixture of both
COOKING TIME: Beans 40–60 minutes; fish and potatoes, a few minutes

*Sacher* POULTRY

# BACKHENDL À LA ANNA SACHER
## (Fried breaded chicken)

### INGREDIENTS

**2 small chickens, about 1–1.2 kg each (with liver) · 200 g flour
300 g bread crumbs · 5 eggs, whisked · peanut oil · 1 bunch parsley · salt**

### PREPARATION

Cut the chicken into pieces, separating the wings and legs, the breast from the back, and halve length-ways. (The neck and back can be used for chicken soup). Leave the bones on the wings and the breast. De-bone the thighs and drumsticks with a small sharp knife. Remove all the skin.

Salt the chicken pieces well, and dredge first in flour then in the beaten egg yolk and finally in the breadcrumbs.

Heat enough oil for deep frying in a pan and wait until it gets very hot. Put the chicken deep enough into the hot oil so the chicken swims. Fry (at about 160 °C) for 20–30 minutes. Turn over once so it fries evenly.

About 15 minutes into frying the chicken, salt and bread the liver and add to the frying pan. Remove the chicken and drain well on kitchen paper. Sprinkle optionally with salt.

Briefly fry the parsley and use to garnish the chicken.

### COOKING TIME: 20–30 minutes
### SUGGESTED SIDE DISHES: Mixed salad

# PAPRIKA CHICKEN

## INGREDIENTS

**1 large chicken or 2 young chickens, ready to cook · 125 ml white wine
1/2 apple, tart (granny smith) · approx. 300 ml chicken stock
150 g onions, chopped · 2 Tbsps paprika powder, sweet
200 ml sour cream · 40 g flour, fine · 150 ml heavy cream · tomato paste
juice and rind from 1/2 lemon · 1/2 chili, seeded, finely chopped
1 bay leaf· 2 Tbsps butter · 4 Tbsps oil · salt · ground pepper
dollop of sour cream for garnish**

## PREPARATION

Wash and quarter the chicken. Separate the spine and neck. Pat dry with kitchen paper. (If the chicken is fatty, remove the skin). Season with salt and pepper.

Heat the oil and butter in a saucepan and lightly fry the chicken pieces (without fillets). Remove, and fry the onions until transparent. Add the tomato paste, paprika powder, and stir. Pour over the wine. Add the chicken stock and then the lemon rind, chili and bay leaf. Bring to boil once and put the drumsticks, neck and back into the pan again. Simmer covered for about 20–25 minutes.

Now add the fillets, and simmer covered for another 20 minutes. Stir regularly and add more stock if necessary. The stock should just cover the chicken.

Remove all the chicken and the bay leaf and keep warm.

Stir the flour into the sour cream until smooth, and then stir it into the sauce with the cream. Chop the apple finely and cook briefly in the sauce. Add lemon juice to taste. Purée the sauce with a handheld mixer and strain through a sieve. Place the chicken (without the neck and back) in the sauce again and briefly heat.

Serve on warmed plates, with an optional dollop of sour cream.

**COOKING TIME:** 40–45 minutes
**SUGGESTED SIDE DISHES:** Dumplings (see veal goulash) or crispy baguette

## "NO MOUNTAIN TOO HIGH ..."

*... recalls long-time Sacher chef Jaroslav Müller. "As a chef you never asked questions about whether a desired dish was 'in', nouvelle cuisine or anything else. You just made it. For example, one time, a Russian minister was visiting and he wanted Chicken Kiev. He got it, even though it wasn't on the menu. Then there was Raoul Castro from Cuba, who wanted something Cuban. I invented a marinated Creole breast of chicken with bitter oranges and black beans especially for him. And he loved it! If the Japanese wanted Congee with salmon for breakfast, of course, they got it, including the miso soup.*

*"Or Lorin Maazel's children. They wanted their hamburgers in buns like you get at McDonald's. What did I do? I sent someone out to McDonald's to get some."*

*Head waiter Reisinger agrees with his former colleague. "There were times when the guests didn't allow the kitchen or the waiters to stipulate anything, let alone suggest anything, the way it is these days. Once someone said he wanted an elephant steak. I told him, 'I'll call Schönbrunn zoo and see if they have some'. So I called, but had to tell my guest, "Sorry, they don't have any'."*

# FREE-RANGE DUCK WITH SEMOLINA DUMPLINGS AND RED CABBAGE AND QUINCE

## INGREDIENTS FOR THE DUCK

1 free-range duck, approx. 2–2.3 kg · 1 onion for the stuffing
1 onion, sliced for frying · 1 apple · one sprig each of marjoram
and savory, plucked · pinch of powdered caraway seeds
300 ml chicken stock · 50 ml sweet wine · salt · ground pepper
cornstarch, optional · grapes for garnish, optional

## 12 SMALL SEMOLINA DUMPLINGS

100 g semolina · 2 Tbsps butter · 1 shallot,
finely chopped · 250 ml milk · 1 egg
1 egg yolk · salt · nutmeg, ground

### FOR THE WALNUT CRUMBING

100 g walnut, grated · 2 Tbsps butter
2 Tbsps breadcrumbs, dark or white bread

### INGREDIENTS FOR THE
### RED CABBAGE AND QUINCE
(marinate a day ahead)

1 kg red cabbage · 1 quince, peeled
2 small apples· 6 cl apple vinegar
200 ml apple juice · 250 ml red wine
1–2 Tbsps cranberries · 1 onion 2 Tbsps
goose dripping (or lard) · 2 Tbsps brown
sugar · 1 bay leaf · salt · ground pepper
caraway seeds, powdered · allspice seeds,
ground · 1 small piece of ginger, peeled
and grated

### PREPARATION FOR THE DUCK

Clean and wash the duck inside and out, and then
salt. For the stuffing, dice the apples and the onion
and combine with pepper, caraway seeds and
the herbs. Stuff inside the cavity of the duck and
close the opening with a pin.

Fill a frying pan with water to the depth of about 1 cm. Place the onion slices and
the duck with breast facing up into the pan. Place in a preheated oven and roast
at 180 °C for 30 minutes. Then baste the duck, leave for about 10 minutes, and
remove from the oven. Cover with foil and roast at 90 °C for another 50 minutes
with the door slightly open. (The meat should loosen and stay juicy and slightly
pink)

Carve the duck, and put under the grill for a few minutes until crispy. Collect
the fat from the grilled duck and, in a pan, use it to sauté the finely chopped
bones along with the stuffing. Pour over the wine and stock and simmer until the
liquid is reduced to about half.

Scrape the fatty residue off the roasting tray, and add to the simmering sauce, pouring over about 300 ml water. Simmer for another 10 minutes.

Strain the liquid through a sieve and taste, adding optional cornstarch and water to bind if necessary. Place the duck, cabbage and dumplings on a warmed plate. Serve with optional sautéed grapes.

COOKING TIME: Duck, roast for 40 minutes at 180 °C; at 90 °C for 50 minutes; grilling time, a few minutes

### PREPARATION FOR THE SEMOLINA DUMPLINGS

Sauté the shallots in butter in a saucepan until transparent. Gradually sprinkle in the semolina, sauté lightly, and add the milk. Season with salt and nutmeg, and stir until the mixture thickens and separates from the pot. Allow to cool slightly. Once the mixture has cooled, add the egg and egg whites, and refrigerate for 20 minutes. With moist hands, form 12 dumplings from the mass and simmer in salt-water on medium heat for about 10 minutes. For the nut-crumbs, heat the butter until it sizzles and add the walnuts and the breadcrumbs. Fry briefly and toss the well-drained dumplings in the crumbs.

COOKING TIME: Approx. 10 minutes

### PREPARATION FOR THE RED CABBAGE AND QUINCE

Before marinating, halve the cabbage, removing the stem and cut finely or slice. Peel and seed the apples and grate coarsely. Combine the cabbage with salt, apples, vinegar, apple juice, wine and cranberries. Cover, and let stand overnight. Slice the onion thinly and sauté in the dripping. Sprinkle in the sugar and melt until light brown in color. Add the cabbage and the marinade, and simmer for about 40 minutes until soft, regularly adding water.

While the cabbage is cooking, peel the quince and cut into 2 mm cubes. Add to the cabbage with the grated ginger, a pinch of powdered caraway, pepper, bay leaf and the allspice seeds. Simmer. Should the cabbage mixture not bind well enough, add some grated potato or water and cornstarch.

COOKING TIME: Approx. 45 minutes

# NAKED IN THE SACHER

*One of the incidents that put the Hotel Sacher foyer in the international media spotlight was undoubtedly the famous press conference that John Lennon and Yoko Ono gave naked from their bed. To avoid possible damage, management had all the valuable paintings removed from the room, one of them being a genuine Defregger.*

*"It wasn't as exciting as the press made it out to be," recalls Sacher's porter Peter Wanninger. "John and Yoko were each wrapped in a sheet when they got into the bed that was set up in the hotel's foyer. Whether they were really naked underneath, nobody can say."*

*The Lennons were extremely decent guests, in contrast with the band the Bee Gees, who, according to Wanninger, "left the Sacher somewhat ravaged".*

## PHEASANT WRAPPED IN BACON WITH CHESTNUT-POTATO DUMPLINGS

### INGREDIENTS

2 pheasants about 1 kg each (perfect skin and carefully plucked)
4 small tart apples, halved · 20 rashes of cold-smoked bacon,
shaved in strips · 2 pieces of one- or two-day old dark bread
5 juniper berries, crushed · 2 small sprigs mountain pine · 200 ml sweet,
tasty white wine · approx. 400 ml chicken stock · 2 small onions, cut
into slices about 1 cm thick · 1 bulb garlic, halved with skin
80 g butter, cold · salt · ground pepper · caraway seeds, powdered
olive oil for frying

### INGREDIENTS FOR THE CHESTNUT-POTATO DUMPLINGS

400 g floury potatoes · 80 g cornstarch (Maizena) · 2 egg yolks
1 egg · 200 g chestnuts, cooked and peeled · 2 Tbsps brown sugar
salt · nutmeg, ground · 2 Tbsps butter · coarse flour for the work surface

## PREPARATION OF THE PHEASANT

Moderately season the well cleaned pheasant inside and out with salt, pepper and caraway seeds (the bacon will provide enough extra taste). Fill with the mountain sprigs and juniper berries. Wrap the pheasant in bacon, tying with thread if necessary. Place the bird, breast down, on top of the bread.

Heat some olive oil in a heavy baking dish, preferably cast iron, and fry the onions, garlic and apples a golden brown. Put the bird with the bread in the dish and roast in a preheated oven at 190 °C, basting it regularly with the chicken stock.

After about 40 minutes, turn the pheasant over, add the wine, and roast for another 20–30 minutes, until done.

Remove the bird from the oven and take the bacon off. Force the apples through a sieve. From the apple cream, use two spoons to form small dumplings. Serve these separately.

Carve the pheasant and arrange on warmed plates. If necessary, add stock to the gravy and allow to boil once. Pass the gravy through a sieve, and bind with cold butter. Pour some gravy over the pheasant and the rest into a gravy boat. Serve with the chestnut-potato dumplings.

**COOKING TIME:** 60–70 minutes
**OVEN TEMPERATURE:** 190 °C in a fan-forced oven

## PREPARATION OF THE CHESTNUT-POTATO DUMPLINGS

Peel the potatoes and boil them in salt water. When still warm, put them through a potato ricer and knead well with the egg yolks, egg, cornstarch, salt and a pinch of nutmeg. Place the dough on a surface dusted with flour. Roll out longish pieces about a finger-width wide. Cut into shorter pieces and shape these into gnocchi-sized dumplings. Using the back of a fork, make gnocchi-like patterns.

Place the dumplings in boiling water and boil for about 2 minutes, drain, and douse with cold water. In a pan, caramelize the brown sugar, add chestnuts and stir well. In a second fry pan, fry the dumplings in butter until golden brown. Mix with the chestnuts, and keep warm in a porcelain bowl.

# MEAT DISHES

*Sacher*

MEAT DISHES

# WIENER SCHNITZEL

## INGREDIENTS

**8 veal cutlets about 90 g each· 4 eggs · 200 g breadcrumbs, very fine 100 g flour, fine · 300 ml butter · 100 ml vegetable or peanut oil · salt lemon slices and fried parsley for garnish**

## PREPARATION

Tenderize the veal to about 2–4 mm, and salt on both sides. On a flat plate, stir the eggs briefly with a fork. (The egg becomes too thin if you beat it too much). Lightly coat the cutlets in flour then dip into the egg, and finally, coat in breadcrumbs. Heat the butter and oil in a large pan (allow the fat to get very hot) and fry the schnitzels until golden brown on both sides. Make sure to toss the pan regularly so that the schnitzels are surrounded by oil and the crumbing becomes 'fluffy'. Remove, and drain on kitchen paper. Fry the parsley in the remaining oil and drain. Place the schnitzels on a warmed plate and serve garnished with parsley and slices of lemon.

**COOKING TIME:** 3–5 minutes

**SUGGESTED SIDE DISHES:** Parsley-tossed potatoes and salad (cucumber, tomato, potato or lettuce)

**TIPS:** Make sure to use high-quality, very fine breadcrumbs. Genuine Wiener schnitzels need to be fried in a frying pan, not in a deep fryer. Also, the use of butter is essential to give the schnitzels a typical 'nutty' taste.

# STUFFED VEAL KIDNEY ROAST

**INGREDIENTS for 6–8 servings**

**2 kg veal loin roast · 1 veal kidney · 6 eggs · 500 g spinach
100 g mushrooms · 1 Tbsp parsley, chopped · 1 sprig each of rosemary
and thyme · flour · 1 tsp tomato paste · 1 Tbsp cream · nutmeg, ground
salt · white ground pepper · butter for frying**

**PREPARATION**

With a sharp knife, separate the meat from all the bones, cutting the inner side so the meat can be folded out (butterfly). Chop the bones into small pieces and mince the meat. Lightly tenderize the butterflied meat.

Beat 5 eggs, stir in some flour, salt and pepper, and make 3 crêpes one after the other in hot butter.

Blanch the spinach briefly in salt water and douse with cold water. Season with salt, pepper and nutmeg.

Remove about half of the fat from the kidneys (some fat should be left on), and quarter.

Slice the mushrooms thinly, and combine with the mince, the rest of the eggs and chopped parsley.

Firstly, place the crêpes on the butterflied meat, then the spinach, kidneys and then the minced meat. Roll it up, and tie together with string. Generously rub salt and pepper into the meat.

Heat the butter in a roasting dish and brown the meat all over. Add the chopped bones and roast in a preheated oven for about 30–40 minutes at 200 °C, basting frequently. Reduce the heat to 140 °C and roast for another 2 hours.

Remove the roast from the dish, cover with foil, and stand for about 20 minutes.

Take the dish, leaving in the bones, and place it on the stove. Stir in the tomato paste and cream. Cook briefly and then dust with a little flour. Add some water and simmer. Strain the sauce, and let simmer again until thick. Remove the string from the meat, and carve.

Place on warmed plates. Pour a little sauce onto the plate and place the meat on top. Pour over a little sauce, and serve the rest of the sauce in a gravy boat.

**COOKING TIME:** Approx. 2 1/2 hours
**OVEN TEMPERATURE:** 200 °C, then 140 °C
**SUGGESTED SIDE DISHES:** Potatoes tossed in parsley; rice and lettuce

salad

# STUFFED BREAST OF VEAL, VIENNESE STYLE

INGREDIENTS for approx. 8–10 servings

**1 breast of veal, approx. 3 kg, pocketed · bones from the breast, finely chopped · 500 ml veal juice · 400 g Kaisersemmeln – type of white bread roll, cubed · 500 ml milk · 100 g melted butter · 6 eggs · 1 Tbsps parsley, chopped · nutmeg, ground · ground pepper· salt · butter for frying**

## PREPARATION

Wash the veal breast and pat dry with kitchen paper. If necessary, widen the pocket opening by hand or with a cooking spoon.

Pour the milk into a bowl and soak the bread roll cubes. Squeeze them out and mix well with melted butter, eggs and chopped parsley. Season with nutmeg, pepper and salt. Fill the veal breast with the stuffing using a spoon. Push firmly into the cavity using a fist. Tightly sew the opening with thread. Rub the outside well with salt and pepper.

Place the chopped bones into a baking dish and put the breast of veal, upside down, on top of the bones. Distribute some generous flakes of butter over the meat. Roast in a preheated oven at 200 °C for about 15 minutes. Baste with the juice, reduce heat to about 160 °C, and roast for another 30 minutes. Turn the breast over and roast for 1 1/2–2 hours

Baste regularly, adding a little water if necessary.

Remove the meat, wrap in greaseproof paper. Leave it to stand for at least 30 minutes in a warm place.

Pour about 250 ml water into the meat juices, mixing in any residue from the dish and simmer well. Drain the fluid.

Carve the meat, and place the slices on warmed plates with a little juice.

**COOKING TIME:** 2 1/2–3 hours
**OVEN TEMPERATURE:** 200 °C, then reduce to 160 °C
**SUGGESTED SIDE DISHES:** Tomato, cucumber or lettuce salad

# MINCED VEAL BUTTER SCHNITZELS

## INGREDIENTS

**600 g veal (cutlets optional), without sinew · 3 Kaisersemmeln, type of white bread roll, without crust · milk for soaking · approx. 200 ml cream 3 egg yolks · 2 tsps breadcrumbs · salt · ground white pepper · nutmeg, ground · grated lemon rind · 50 g butter · 3 Tbsps oil · veal juice or soup for garnishing**

## PREPARATION

Soak the white part of the bread rolls in the milk. Roughly cube the meat, and mince along with the soaked bread.

Combine egg yolk, salt, pepper, nutmeg and a little lemon rind in a bowl. Mix in the cream and breadcrumbs and refrigerate.

Form smallish patties from the meat/bread mixture. Heat oil in a teflon-lined, oven-proof pan and briefly fry on each side. Add butter and allow to melt. Place the pan in the preheated oven and bake for about 10 minutes at 160 °C.

Serve on warmed plates with warm veal juice or a little soup.

**COOKING TIME:** Depending on the size of the patties, 10–12 minutes
**SUGGESTED SIDE DISHES:**
Rice with peas, mashed potatoes and
cucumber salad

# FRIED VEAL LIVER, VIENNESE STYLE

## INGREDIENTS

**800 g veal liver · 5–8 small shallots · 250 g small mushrooms 3 Tbsps finely chopped shallots for the liver · 200 g streaky bacon in strips · 400 ml stock · 30 ml apple vinegar · 40 g butter for binding flour and butter mixture for thickening · vegetable oil for frying salt · ground pepper · fresh marjoram leaves**

## PREPARATION

Slice the mushrooms. Cut shallots length-wise and sauté in hot vegetable oil. Add the mushrooms and lightly sauté. Add the strips of bacon and fry briefly. Season

with salt and pepper and keep warm.

Clean the liver (remove skin and veins) and slice thinly. Heat the oil in a teflon-lined frying pan and fry, tossing regularly. Be careful not to over-fry, otherwise the liver will become hard. Add the shallots, and sauté. Remove the liver from the pan and place on a plate. Rinse the frying pan juices with vinegar, add the stock, and simmer. Add the liver again, seasoning with salt and pepper. Toss the contents of the pan and then bind with cold butter. (If necessary, add a little flour and butter to thicken the sauce).

Arrange on warmed plates with the mushroom-bacon mix. Garnish with marjoram leaves.

**COOKING TIME:** 3–4 minutes
**SUGGESTED GARNISH:** Blanched and sautéed mushroom caps
**SUGGESTED SIDE DISHES:** Fried potatoes (see Tafelspitz)

# TAFELSPITZ (Boiled Beef)
# WITH CLASSIC SIDE DISHES

## INGREDIENTS for 6 servings

1 round of beef, approx. 2 kg (with a little fat) · approx. 750 g beef bones
3 carrots · 3 turnips/parsnips · 1 small celeriac · 1 onion · 2 bay leaves
10 peppercorns · 2 juniper berries · salt · chopped chives for decoration

## PREPARATION

Fill a large pot with about 5 liters of cold water. Wash the bones and boil in the water. Remove the sinew and skin from the beef but leave the fat on. Place the meat, bay leaves, peppercorns and juniper berries in the water and simmer just below boiling point on low heat for about 2–2 1/2 hours, regularly skimming off the fat.

Halve the unpeeled onion, and fry, without fat, preferably in old pan, on the cut surface until dark brown.

Cut the vegetables into large cubes and add with the onion to the meat. Simmer for another hour until the meat is really tender. (Test the meat with a fork to see if it's ready: the fork should slide in easily when the meat is ready).

Remove the meat, strain the soup, and put the meat back in the soup for a while. Take note: as long as the meat is sitting in the soup, don't add salt, otherwise it will become red and dry up.

Slice the meat, and arrange on a warmed plate. Pour over a little soup, add salt to taste, and sprinkle with chives. Serve with extra-crispy fried potatoes, chive sauce and apple-horseradish sauce.

COOKING TIME: Depending on the quality of the beef, 3–3 1/2 hours

# TAFELSPITZ WITHOUT MEAT

*Long-serving chefs still rave about the 700 to 800 kilo oxen that, in contrast with today, were available and easy to come by in the Fifties and Sixties. It was the kind of meat that gave the Tafelspitz a veritable, two-inch layer of fat. This was a favorite for some regular guests. One of them, the count of Fürstenberg, always ordered his Tafelspitz "without meat", and sometimes ate the fat with freshly-ground pepper.*

# CLASSIC TAFELSPITZ SIDE DISHES:

## FRIED POTATOES

### INGREDIENTS

**600–700 g potatoes · 2–3 Tbsps vegetable oil or dripping
ground nutmeg · salt**

### PREPARATION

Boil the potatoes until soft. Peel while still warm and use a slicer to cut into fine slices.

Heat the oil or dripping in a pan. Fry the potatoes until golden brown, seasoning with salt and nutmeg. Drain on kitchen paper before serving.

**COOKING TIME:** Boil for 15–18 minutes; fry for approx. 10 minutes

## CHIVE SAUCE

### INGREDIENTS FOR 6 SERVINGS

**2 boiled eggs · 100 ml vegetable oil · 2 pieces of toast, without crust
250 ml milk · 250 g sour cream · 2 Tbsps chives, finely chopped
salt · white pepper**

### PREPARATION

Soak the toast in milk. Peel and cut the eggs. Drain the toast, and mix with the eggs and other ingredients using a hand-held mixer.

Season the sauce to taste and allow to cool. Serve in a gravy boat.

## APPLE-HORSERADISH SAUCE

### INGREDIENTS

**3–4 tart apples (granny smiths) · 1 Tbsp icing sugar · 2 cl lemon juice ·
approx. 30 g fresh horseradish, grated (or horseradish from a jar)
salt · a few drops of beef stock**

### PREPARATION

Peel the apples and cut into slices. Remove seeds. Grate the apples, quickly adding lemon juice and mix well with the rest of the ingredients.

# BEEF ROULADE

INGREDIENTS for 8 servings
8 rounds beef schnitzel (use ox meat), 150 g each · 2 Tbsps hot English
mustard · 3 onions, cut lengthways · 2 ripe tomatoes · 200 ml Burgunder
(or other full-bodied red wine) · 1.2 l vegetable/beef stock or water
2 juniper berries, lightly pressed · 1 bay leaf· 1 vinegar gherkin, finely
chopped · grated lemon rind · 40 ml vegetable oil for frying · flour
salt · ground pepper · capers · sprigs of thyme for garnish

FOR THE STUFFING
2 carrots · 1 turnip · 1 bunch parsley, leaves plucked · 16 quail eggs
(or 3 normal eggs) · 8 slices prosciutto (or other cured ham)

FOR THE FRIED ONIONS
2 white onions · salt · a pinch of paprika powder · 50–100 g flour, coarse
Peanut oil for frying

PREPARATION
Peel the carrots and turnip and cut thinly lengthways. Blanch in salt water, douse
in cold water, and drain.
Boil the quail eggs for 3 minutes, douse in cold water and carefully peel. (When
using normal eggs, boil, then peel and quarter).
Cover the beef with plastic wrap and lightly tenderize. Season with salt and
pepper, and spread mustard on one side. Cover first with prosciutto, then some
vegetables (keep some for the sauce) and parsley. Place the eggs in the middle
of the meat and roll the fillet into a roulade. Pin together with toothpicks. Season
with salt and pepper, dust with flour and fry all over quickly in vegetable oil.
Remove, and fry the onions and the rest of the vegetables in the fat. Add the halved
tomato, and fry, then pour on the red wine. Simmer until the vegetables are soft.
Add the bay leaf and berries, pour in the stock and place the roulade in the sauce.
Roast in a preheated oven at 180 °C for 50–90 minutes (depending on the meat).
Baste regularly.
When the roulade is done, remove from the oven, and wrap in foil. Keep warm.
Add the finely-chopped gherkin and lemon rind to the sauce and simmer
vigorously. Strain the sauce, and season to taste. If it is too thin, add a little water
and flour.
Place the roulade in the sauce and let draw for a about 10 minutes. Garnish the
roulade with thyme and capers.

**COOKING TIME:** 1–1 1/2 hours, depending on the meat
**SUGGESTED SIDE DISHES:** Mashed potatoes with fried onions. (For the fried onions, slice the onions thinly with a breadcutting machine. Lightly salt, sprinkle with paprika and toss in flour. Place in a large sieve and shake off extra flour. Heat oil in a pan and fry the onions until golden brown. Remove, and drain on some paper towel).

# SIRLOIN WITH ONIONS, FRIED POTATOES AND GHERKIN MUSTARD

### INGREDIENTS
**4 short loin, approx. 180 g each · 4 shallots**
**400 ml veal juice · 200 ml bouillon**
**100 ml vegetable oil· 2 cl apple vinegar**
**cold butter for binding · flour**
**English mustard · salt · ground pepper**

### INGREDIENTS FOR THE FRIED POTATOES
**600 g potatoes · butter for frying · caraway seeds · salt**

### INGREDIENTS FOR GHERKIN MUSTARD
**200 g mustard gherkins · 80 g Pommery mustard**
**1 Tbsp English mustard · grated lemon rind · 2 Tbsps capers**
**1 Tbsp honey · 1 anchovy ring · salt · ground pepper**

### PREPARATION FOR THE SIRLOIN
Clean the meat well and make small cuts into the top of the meat so that it doesn't bulge during roasting. Tenderize with a meat hammer. Season with salt and pepper, and spread with mustard. Dredge the meat on one side with flour.
Heat the oil in a large pan. Brown the meat briefly on the floured side first, then, just as quickly, fry the other side. Remove from the pan and keep warm.
Cut the shallots in strips, add to the pan and sauté until brown. Pour in the veal juice, apple vinegar and bouillon, and let it reduce somewhat. Stir in some butter to bind.

Arrange the meat on a plate, pour over some sauce and serve with potatoes. Serve the gherkin mustard separately.

**COOKING TIME:** 3–4 minutes
**SUGGESTED GARNISH:** Crispy fried onions

**PREPARATION FOR THE POTATOES**
Cut or slice the raw, peeled potatoes and boil until soft in salt-caraway seed water for 15–18 minutes, then drain. Fry in hot butter until golden brown. Add salt to taste before serving.

**PREPARATION OF THE GHERKIN MUSTARD**
(keeps for 14 days)
Cut the gherkins into small, fine cubes. Chop the anchovy roll and capers very finely and mix all the ingredients well. Refrigerate.

# SIRLOIN À LA ESTERHÁZY

## INGREDIENTS

4 pieces of short sirloin approx. 180–200 g each · root vegetables
(parsnips, turnips carrots)
1 large onion · 50 g rashes bacon · 1 cooking spoon capers
Estragon mustard
125 ml cream · 125 g sour cream · 100 ml white wine · 300 ml beef stock
rind from 1/2 lemon · 1 bay leaf · 20 g flour, fine · salt · ground pepper
Butter for sautéing · oil for frying · parsley for decoration

## PREPARATION

Slice finely in strips the onion, bacon and vegetables. Chop the capers finely. Cover the sirloin with plastic wrap and tenderize until thin. Cut the edges of the meat with a sharp knife so that the meat doesn't split when cooked.

Season the meat with salt and pepper and spread with mustard. Heat oil in a large pan, letting it get very hot. Brown the meat on both sides. Remove from the pan, and fry the bacon and onions in the fat. Pour over the white wine, and let cook for a while. Add beef stock and simmer. Replace the meat. Add the lemon rind, capers and bay leaf. Simmer covered (preferably in the oven at 180 °C) for about 1 1/2 hours until tender. Make sure to turn regularly.

Sauté the vegetables in lightly foaming butter.

As soon as the meat is done, remove from the pan along with the bay leaf and keep warm.

Combine the sour cream, cream and flour and stir until smooth. Mix into the sauce. Simmer until thick and most of the liquid has evaporated. Add the vegetables to the sauce, stir well, and season to taste.

Arrange the sirloin on warmed plates, pour over the sauce, and sprinkle over some parsley.

**COOKING TIME:** 1 1/2 hours
**OVEN TEMPERATURE:** 180 °C
**SUGGESTED SIDE DISHES:**
Bread dumplings (see Beuschel, p. 53)

# SILVERWARE AS WITNESS TO THE CROWN

*If only the silver soup tureens, the candelabras and cutlery from the cutlery chamber of the Hotel Sacher could talk. Perhaps they could also tell us the truth about the Mayerling tragedy.*

*Unlike his father, the ascetic emperor and strict follower of customs, Crown Prince Rudolf was a regular guest at the Sacher Hotel, even if he was infamously known there for not paying his bills.*

*Following his suicide in Mayerling, Anna Sacher respectfully allowed enough time to pass before sending the long-outstanding tab to the Viennese court. She let them know, however, that instead of cash she would accept a few nice pieces of Mayerling's silver tableware, which was now without owner.*

*And this is how the silver from the execrated castle in the Wienerwald ended up in the noble hotel behind the State Opera – where it is in constant use, is cherished, and lovingly cleaned.*

# OLD VIENNESE-STYLE ROAST PORK WITH FRIED POTATOES

### INGREDIENTS FOR 8 SERVINGS
1 pork tender loin approx. 2 kg · 8 shallots, halved
16 medium potatoes, halved · 1–1.5 l vegetable stock or water
24 cloves garlic, crushed, with skin · 8 carrots, halved length-wise

### FOR THE PASTE
3 Tbsp mineral salt · 2 cloves garlic, blanched
2 Tbsp coarsely ground pepper · 1 cooking spoon caraway seeds, whole · rind from 1/2 lemon, grated · 4 juniper berries
2 Tbsp melted pork dripping or vegetable oil

### PREPARATION
Using a pestle and mortar, mash all the ingredients for the paste. Rub the paste well into the meat. Place in a cast iron oven dish and add the shallots and garlic. Roast

in the oven at 220 °C for about 20 minutes. Turn regularly.

Lightly blanche the carrots and potatoes, douse in cold water and add to the roast. After about 20 minutes, pour in 400 ml stock and roast for another 40 minutes. Keep basting with juices from the dish (if there's not enough liquid, add more stock).

As soon as the carrots, potatoes and garlic are soft, take them out of the oven and cover them with foil. After about 90–100 minutes the meat should be done. To test, use a needle or prong: It will be done when only juice oozes out, no blood.

Remove from the oven and cover with foil for about 20 minutes. In a pan, toss the vegetables in a little roasting juice.

Carve the meat and arrange on a plate with the potatoes and vegetables. Add a little stock to the juice, strain, and simmer for a few minutes. Season to taste and serve with the meat.

**COOKING TIME:** 90–100 minutes
**OVEN TEMPERATURE:** 220 °C
**SUGGESTED SIDE DISHES:** Bread dumplings (see Beuschel, p. 53)
**TIP:** Shortly before the meat is done, pour some dark beer over the meat. It adds a wonderful aroma to the gravy.

# ROAST LAMB IN A
# POTATO FRITTER JACKET (Rösti)

### INGREDIENTS

400–600 g lamb fillets · 500 g floury potatoes · 150 g chicken fillet
2 red peppers, vitamized (or braised in oil and puréed)
300 g green beans · Tabasco sauce · pinch of sugar · 1 Tbsp cornstarch
(Maizena) · 100 g cream, cold · 1 egg · 1 Tbsp basil pesto · 1 Tbsp butter
Vegetable oil · salt · nutmeg, grated · ground pepper
Thyme for garnishing

## PREPARATION

Peel the potatoes and either grate or cut length-wise into very fine strips. Salt well and leave to sit for about 5 minutes, then squeeze out the juice. Add the nutmeg and cornstarch and make 8 thin patties from the mass (approx. 12 cm Ø).

Heat the vegetable oil, and place the patties into the pan, press flat and fry a golden brown. Drain well on kitchen paper and, with a round cutter, cut pieces about 10 cm Ø from the patties. Allow to cool.

For the stuffing, cut the chicken fillet into small cubes and mix with the cold cream, salt and egg. Push through a colander or sieve and spread some stuffing thinly onto 4 of the fritters.

Cut the lamb fillet into slices about 1 cm thick and season with the pesto, salt and pepper. Place the fillets on the fritter and spread a thin layer of stuffing over the meat. Spread the rest of the stuffing over the fritters and place these, stuffing side down, on the meat. Press down and shape roundly over the top of the meat.

In a teflon-lined pan, heat vegetable oil and fry the patties a golden brown on each side. Place a rack into the roasting dish and put the meat on top. Roast for 10 minutes in a preheated, fan-forced oven at 165 °C. Remove and cover with foil. Allow to stand for 8 minutes.

In the meantime, simmer the juice from the peppers until it reduces to a third. Stir in 4 tablespoons of olive oil, salt, Tabasco sauce and sugar, making a thick sauce.

Cook the beans al dente in salt water and toss in butter. Season with salt and pepper and arrange on warmed plates. Cut the "rösti burger" in half, and arrange on the plates. Pour over sauce to serve. Garnish with thyme.

### COOKING TIME:

Approx. 10 minutes in the oven

### OVEN TEMPERATURE:

165 °C in a fan-forced oven

*Sacher*

# VENISON WITH ROWAN BERRIES AND CHESTNUT PEARS

## INGREDIENTS

**600 g fillets from a rack of venison, cut into 8 medallions · 50 ml Madeira · 50 ml brandy 1 small chunk bitter chocolate · 400 ml meat juice from venison (or veal) · dried mugwort, grated 4 Tbsp rowan berries, soaked in sugar syrup 2 cl Trester schnaps or rowan berry brandy 2 Williams pears, not too ripe · 2 Tbsps cold butter for the sauce · 2 Tbsps butter for the pears 2 Tbsps brown sugar · lemon juice · 12 chestnuts, roasted and peeled · salt · ground pepper 2 Tbsps olive oil · 1 Tbsp butter for the medallions**

## PREPARATION

After cutting medallions from the rack, tie each one with thread. Season with salt and pepper, and fry briefly in olive oil. Keep warm in a preheated oven at 80 °C.

For the sauce, simmer the Madeira and brandy until the liquid is reduced by half. Pour in the meat juice and simmer until liquid reduces to 200 ml. Add the mugwort and salt to taste. Stir in the chocolate and bind with the cold butter. Keep warm.

Peel and halve the pears. Remove the seeds. From the pear halves, cut length-wise (see photo) and fry golden brown in butter and sugar. Dribble over some lemon juice and add the chestnuts. Toss well.

Warm up the rowan berries in some syrup and Trester schnaps.

Fry the medallions in butter. Place the meat and pears on warmed plates, with the chestnuts on top of the pears. Pour over the sauce and sprinkle with berries. Garnish with mugwort.

**COOKING TIME:** A few minutes frying; simmering time, 8–10 minutes
**OVEN TEMPERATURE:** 80 °C
**SUGGESTED SIDE DISHES:** Celeriac, Topinambur purée or steamed Brussels sprout leaves

# GAME À LA WALT DISNEY

*How do you explain to an American what 'Rehpastete' is?*
*When Walt Disney was in Vienna, the head waiter Robert Palfrader found out just how hard that was.*
*"It's a pie of venison," he said, not knowing that Americans don't use the word 'venison'.*
*"You mean deer?" asked Disney.*
*"No, deer is … a 'Hirsch'," the confused head waiter said.*
*Suddenly he found the right explanation: "It's a pie of Bambi!" he exclaimed.*
*Walt Disney immediately understood. And ordered something else.*

Sacher

# COLD DESSERTS

# MARBLE GUGELHUPF

## INGREDIENTS

**200 g butter · 100 g icing sugar · 100 g sugar · 4 egg yolks
4 egg whites · 230 g flour, fine · 20 g cocoa powder · vanilla sugar
pinch of salt · butter and flour for the baking mold
icing sugar for dusting**

## PREPARATION

Beat the butter, icing sugar and vanilla sugar and a pinch of salt until fluffy. Gradually stir in the egg yolks. Whisk the egg whites with the sugar until stiff and fold into the egg yolk mixture. Mix in the flour. Color about a third of the mixture with cocoa.

Grease the gugelhupf basin with butter, and dust with flour. Now fill the form alternately with the light and dark mixture. Bake in a preheated oven at 180 °C for about one hour.

Overturn the cake onto a cake rack and allow to cool. Sprinkle with icing sugar.

**BAKING TIME:** Approx. 1 hour
**OVEN TEMPERATURE:** 180 °C

# SACHER TORTE

*The recipe for the famous original Sacher Torte is kept in a safe in the Sacher hotel and is guarded like a treasure. The following recipe is a simplified version from the Sacher's head confectioner. When made correctly, it comes as close to the original as you'll ever get.*

## INGREDIENTS FOR A CAKE FORM 22–24 CM Ø

**140 g butter, room temperature · 110 g icing sugar
pulp from 1/2 vanilla pod · 6 egg yolks · 6 egg whites
130 g eating chocolate · 110 g sugar · 140 g flour, fine
approx. 200 g apricot jam · butter and flour for the
cake form · whipped cream**

## FOR THE FROSTING

**200 g sugar · 125 ml water · 150 g chocolate**

## PREPARATION

In a bowl, whip the butter, icing sugar and vanilla pulp until creamy. Gradually add the egg yolks, and continue beating until the mixture is thick and creamy.

Melt the chocolate in a bain-marie (double boiler). When completely melted, fold into the mass. Beat the egg white until stiff, sprinkling in the sugar and continue to beat until the mass is stiff and glossy. Heap the beaten egg white onto the egg yolk mixture, sift over the flour and carefully fold with a cooking spoon.

Line the bottom of a spring-clip cake form with baking paper and grease the sides of the form with butter. Sift over some flour. Fill the spring form with the mixture and spread evenly. Bake in a preheated oven at 170 °C for 55–60 minutes, leaving the door slightly ajar during the first 10–15 minutes. (You can test the cake to see if it's done by pressing lightly on it with your finger. There should be slight resistance).

Still in the cake form, turn the cake upside down on a cake rack and allow to cool for about 20 minutes. Open up the spring form and peel off the paper. Put the form back on the cake, then turn the cake over, and allow to fully cool in the form so that all the unevenness can settle and smooth out on the surface.

Remove the cake form and cut the cake in half horizontally with a sharp knife.

Warm up the jam, stir until smooth and spread on to both cake halves, then put back together again. Spread the jam all over the cake and allow to dry a little.

For the frosting, bring the water and sugar to boil so that it bubbles for about 5–6 minutes. Allow to cool slightly. Melt the chocolate in a bain-marie and, stirring, gradually add the sugar until it becomes a thick glaze. (See 'Tips'). Quickly pour the slightly warm frosting over the cake and, with a spatula, spread the frosting smoothly over the surface of the cake.

Allow to dry for a few hours, until the icing is hard. Serve with whipped cream.

**BAKING TIME:** 55–60 minutes

**OVEN TEMPERATURE:** 170 °C

**SUGGESTED DECORATION:** Usually the Sacher Torte isn't decorated. Only in the house of Sacher does it get a 'cake stamp'.

**TIP:** To test the correct consistency of the frosting, pour some over a wooden cooking spoon. A layer of icing about 4 cm thick should stick to the spoon. Should the icing be too thick, it can be thinned by adding a few drops of sugar water (use what is left from the water-sugar mix and dissolve with a little water). Also, make sure that the icing doesn't get too hot, otherwise it will be matt when it dries, and not glossy.

# THE SACHER TORTE:
# A PART OF THE VIENNESE WAY OF LIFE

*"It's our 'door opener'",* says Elisabeth Gürtler about the famous Sacher Torte. *"It's known all over the world."*

In fact, apart from the Danube waltz, Amadeus, the Lipizzaner horses, Sisi and the Sängerknaben, there is hardly any other homemade trademark that is as widely recognized as the Sacher Torte.

*"The beauty of it is that it can be a given as a gift and you can say it's much more than just a cake,"* says Gürtler.

For years now the Sacher Torte has been a symbol of the Viennese way of life and lust for life all over the world. The success story began with the cake's creator Franz Sacher in the Biedermeir period when he was working as an apprentice chef for Count Metternich. The count's cook fell ill just when a new dessert was needed.

*"Be sure not to bring shame on me tonight!"* is what the Austrian State Chancellor, Prince Klemens Wenzel von Metternich, is said to have cautioned the young man back in 1832.

Since then, many stories have developed about how the original Sacher Torte was actually created. One of them says that a panicked Franz Sacher was advised by his sister – who later became the licensee at the Nußdorfer Spitz. But that's debatable. Another rumor says that Franz Sacher was an apprentice at the confectioners Dehne (which later became Demel) but cannot be founded on historical grounds.

Historical circumstances have shown that the original Sacher Torte was made every day until 1998. As a bakery, a basement vault in the hotel was used, which, as Elisabeth Gürtler recalls, demanded *"an adventurous kind of improvisation"*. Sacks of sugar and blocks of chocolate had to be carried down the spiral staircase by daylight, and a cake kitchen without ventilation was created in the basement. The finished cakes (today 350,000 per year) were packed and transported upstairs via the same stairs.

In the meantime, the Sacher Torte is made in facilities especially built for the production of the cake not far from the hotel. Apart from small, necessary alterations in keeping with today's consciousness about nutrition, Franz Sacher's original recipe has remained the same since 1832.

# ESTERHÁZY TORTE

INGREDIENTS FOR 1 CAKE FORM, 24 CM Ø

8 egg whites · 200 g icing sugar · rind from 1 lemon, grated · a pinch
of powdered cinnamon · 150 g almonds, grated finely with skin
40 g flour, fine · 300 ml milk · 150 g sugar · pulp from 1 vanilla pod
40 g vanilla custard powder · 3 egg yolks · 2 cl cherry brandy
300 g butter · 80 g apricot jam · 2 cl rum · 300 g fondant (thick,
white sugar glaze) · cocoa · 2–3 Tbsps shaved almonds, roasted

## PREPARATION

Preheat the oven to 180 °C

Whisk the egg white with 2/3 of the icing sugar until half stiff, then add the lemon
rind, cinnamon and the rest of the sugar, and keep whisking until the mass is stiff
and glossy. Carefully fold in the almonds and the sifted flour.

Draw 6 circles about 24 cm Ø on baking paper. Spread each of them thinly with
the cake mixture. In batches, bake each one light brown in a hot oven with the door

partially open for 8–10 minutes. Loosen the bottom of each cake from the paper with a spatula and then allow to cool.

For the cream filling, beat the butter until creamy. Heat about 2/3 of the milk with the sugar and vanilla pulp. Use the rest of the milk to mix with the custard powder, egg yolks and cherry brandy. Stir until smooth, then combine with the milk mixture. Allow to cool. Spoon the cooled custard into the creamy butter mixture, and stir until it becomes a smooth butter cream.

Spread the cream over five of the cake layers and place them on top of each other, keeping some cream for the end. Put the 6th layer upside down on a bench surface. Heat the jam and rum and spread over the bottom. Warm the fondant to body temperature (no hotter than 40 °C) and pour, slightly cooled, over the layer spread with jam (6th layer), keeping about 2-3 tablespoons for the decorative pattern. Quickly smooth over with a spatula.

Place this layer on top of the cake and spread the sides of the cake with the rest of the butter cream. Apply the shaved almonds to the sides of the cake.

For the typical Esterházy decorative pattern, stir some cocoa into the fondant and fill into a pastry bag. At a distance of about 2 cm, squeeze out semi circles and quickly take the back of a knife and pull it across perpendicularly from alternate sides. (See photo for pattern).

Allow to stand for a while before cutting.

**BAKING TIME: 8–10 MINUTES**
**OVEN TEMPERATURE:** 180 °C

# MALAKOV CHOCOLATE TORTE

## INGREDIENTS FOR 1 CAKE 24 CM Ø
**approx. 50 lady fingers**

### FOR THE CAKE
**1/2 tub (= 125 g) sour cream · 1/2 cup sugar · 1/2 cup walnuts, ground 1/2 cup cocoa · 1/2 cup flour, fine · 1/2 cooking spoon baking powder 65 ml Canola · 1 egg · 1 egg yolk · butter for greasing**

### FOR THE VANILLA CREAM
**350 ml milk · 60 g sugar · 30 g vanilla custard · 300 ml cream, half whipped · 4 sheets gelatin · pulp from 1 vanilla pod · pinch of salt**

### FOR THE CHOCOLATE CREAM
**200 g bitter couverture (at least 60 % cocoa content) · 180 ml milk 3 sheets gelatin · 300 ml heavy cream, half whipped**

### FOR SOAKING
**250 ml sugarwater (water and sugar 1:1 boiled) · 100 ml rum**

### FOR THE DECORATION
**200 ml cream, whipped · approx. 150 g shaved almonds, roasted 100 g orange or apricot jam · macaroons or halved ladyfingers**

### PREPARATION

For the cake, mix all the ingredients together with a slotted spoon until smooth. Grease a spring-clip cake form with butter. Pour in the mixture and bake in a preheated oven at 180 °C for about 10–12 minutes. Allow to cool, then take off the spring form.

For the vanilla cream, stir the custard powder into 3–4 tablespoons of cold milk. Soak the gelatin in cold water. Heat the rest of the milk with the vanilla pulp, sugar and a pinch of salt. Mix in the custard and stir until the mixture is thick. Remove from the stove, and mix in the drained gelatin with a hand mixer. Cool to room temperature, and then fold in the half-whipped cream.

For the chocolate cream, soak the gelatin, chop up the chocolate and place in a bowl. Heat up the milk and pour over the chocolate. Mix in the drained gelatin with a hand mixer until the mixture becomes elastic. Cool to body temperature, and then fold in the half-whipped cream.

Place the cake in another spring form of the same size. Combine the sugarwater with rum and dribble some over the cake. Warm up the jam and spread over the cake. Then spread about 2 cm of chocolate cream over the jam. Dip the ladyfingers briefly in the soaking mixture and place on top of the chocolate layer. Spread a layer of vanilla cream about 2 cm thick over the ladyfingers and cover again with ladyfingers. Repeat the process until all the creams are used up, and finish with the vanilla cream. Smooth the cream on all sides and allow to cool for about 3 hours.

Carefully remove the cake form, and spread the cake very thinly with whipped cream. Apply the almonds to the sides of the cake. Decorate the top of the cake with cream roses and with optional macaroons or halved ladyfingers.

**BAKING TIME:** 10–12 minutes
**OVEN TEMPERATURE:** 180 °C

# CARDINAL SLICES

FOR THE FIRST MIXTURE

350 g egg white · 240 g icing sugar· 1 tsp vanilla sugar · pinch of salt
Icing sugar for dusting

FOR THE SECOND MIXTURE

3 eggs · 4 egg yolks · 80 g icing sugar · lemon rind, grated · 75 g flour, fine

FOR THE THIRD MIXTURE

400 ml cream · 2 sheets gelatin · 40 g icing sugar · 2 Tbsps instant coffee
2 cl advocat · pinch of salt · 300 g fresh raspberries · 3 cl raspberry
brandy · 1 handful shaved almonds, roasted

PREPARATION

For the first mixture, beat the egg whites, icing sugar, vanilla sugar and salt until
the mixture is thick and stiff.

For the second mixture, beat the eggs with the yolks, icing sugar and lemon rind
until fluffy. Fold in the flour. Cut out two strips of baking paper (14 x 35 cm), and
place on a baking tray. Fill a frosting bag with a large, round nozzle and fill it with
the mixture. On each piece of baking paper squeeze out 3 lines about 2 cm apart.
Do the same with the egg white mixture, squeezing these lines between the first
mixture. Sprinkle generously with icing sugar.

Place in a preheated oven and bake at 180 °C with the door slightly open (the
mass should dry). Allow to cool, then turn upside down on a platter and remove
the baking paper.

For the third mixture, marinate the raspberries in brandy. Whip the cream with the
instant coffee until stiff. Soak and drain the gelatin. Heat up the advocat and stir in
the gelatin until it dissolves. Stir into the cream along with the icing sugar and salt.
Allow to thicken in a cool place.

Fill half of the mixture into a pastry bag and squeeze onto the first base. Place
the marinated raspberries on top, and squeeze on the rest of the mixture. Place
the second base on top of the cream, and sprinkle with almonds and icing sugar.
Cut into slices with a sharp knife.

BAKING TIME: 20–25 minutes
OVEN TEMPERATURE: 180 °C

# SWISS ROLL

### INGREDIENTS FOR 8 SERVINGS

**5 egg whites · 4 egg yolks · 20 g butter, melted· 70 g sugar
40 g flour, fine · 40 g cornstarch · 1 tsps vanilla sugar · pinch of salt
250 g apricot jam · 4 cl apricot brandy · icing sugar for dusting**

### PREPARATION

Place the cold egg whites in a cold bowl and, using a mixer on medium level, beat the sugar, vanilla sugar and salt until the mixture is creamy. Make sure it doesn't become fluffy. Then fold in the egg yolks. Stir in the butter and carefully fold in the sifted cornstarch.

Spread the mass about a finger-width thick on a baking tray lined with baking paper. Shape and smooth so that it becomes an even square. Bake in a preheated oven at 220 °C for 8–10 minutes until the surface just begins to dry. Remove from oven, and turn upside down (with baking paper still on) onto a tea towel or baking paper dusted with icing sugar. Carefully peel off the baking paper. Briefly heat up the jam, stir in the apricot brandy and spread over the cake. Carefully roll up the cake and wrap in baking paper, and leave it to cool. Remove the paper and dust generously with icing sugar.

**BAKING TIME:** 8–10 minutes
**OVEN TEMPERATURE:** 220 °C

# PLUM CAKE WITH HAZELNUT CRUMBLE

**300 g flour, fine · 25 g moist yeast · salt · 3 egg yolks
1 cooking spoon vanilla sugar · 30 g sugar · 100 ml milk
rind from 1/2 lemon, grated · 40 g melted butter · 20–25 small plums,
quartered and pitted · 150 g plum or apricot jam · 4 cl rum or
old plum brandy · icing sugar for dusting · flour for the work surface**

**120 g flour · 100 g sugar · 100 g butter · 60 g raw marzipan
60 g hazelnuts, roasted and ground · salt · 1 cooking spoon
vanilla sugar · pinch of cinnamon**

Heat the milk to 30 °C. Crumble in the yeast and stir well. Add the egg yolk, vanilla sugar and sugar, flour, a pinch of salt and the lemon rind. Stir in the melted butter and, using a blender or mixer, mix until it becomes a smooth dough. Cover and leave to rise for 40 minutes. On a floured surface, knead thoroughly. Cover and leave to rise again for about 30 minutes.

For the crumble, knead all the ingredients together well, shape into a roll, wrap in foil and leave to sit for 1 hour in a cool place.

Line a baking tray with baking paper. Roll out the dough about 8 mm thick to about 30 x 50 cm. Place on the baking tray, spread with warmed jam and, pressing them slightly into the dough, lay the plums with cut side facing up. Dribble over some rum or plum brandy. With a vegetable grater, coarsely grate over the crumble mixture and let sit for 20 minutes.

Bake golden brown in a preheated, fan-forced oven at 190 °C for 30–40 minutes. Dust with icing sugar when still warm.

**BAKING TIME:** 30–40 minutes
**OVEN TEMPERATURE:** 190 °C in a fan-forced oven

# CREAM SLICES

## INGREDIENTS FOR APPROX. 12 SLICES

**400 g pastry (home or ready-made) · 6 sheets gelatin · 5 egg yolks
3 eggs · 80 g sugar · 1 Tbsps vanilla sugar · 4 cl rum · pinch of salt
500 ml cream, whipped · pulp from 1 vanilla pod · apricot jam
Fondant for frosting/glaze · flour for the work surface**

## PREPARATION

Soak the gelatin in cold water. Firstly over a double boiler, then cold, beat the vanilla pulp, egg yolks, eggs, both sugars, rum and salt until fluffy. Drain the gelatin, heat up in about 50 ml water, and add to the mass. Carefully fold in the whipped cream.

Fill a 30 x 20 cm sized square baking tray with the vanilla-cream mixture and allow to cool.

Roll out the pastry on a floured surface to about the thickness of knife handle and cut out two 30 x 20 cm squares. Place on a baking tray lined with baking paper, pierce several times with a fork and let sit. Bake in a preheated oven at 180 °C for 15–20 minutes. Allow to cool.

Spread warmed apricot jam over the smooth side of the pastry. Heat the fondant to about 40 °C and brush onto one of the pieces of pastry. Allow to dry at about 60 °C. From the baking tray, turn the cream upside down onto the unglazed piece of pastry. Place the glazed piece of pastry on top. Cut into slices.

**BAKING TIME:** 15–20 minutes
**OVEN TEMPERATURE:** 180 °C

## SWEET POISON

*Director of the Sacher, Reiner Heilmann, who is also responsible for the production of the Sacher Torte, sometimes receives letters from people with complaints about the Sacher Torte, though it doesn't happen often.*

*"The most memorable letter of complaint I've had in my time at the Sacher was worded rather strongly," recalls Heilmann. It was from an Austrian living abroad. He complained that the package was labeled 'Gift Parcel' ('poisoned parcel' in German), and said there was no way he could give it to anyone as a gift.*

*As with the recipe for the Sacher Torte, the following is also not the original recipe for the Sacher cubes, but a simplified version. It still makes an excellent recipe.*

# SACHER CUBES

### INGREDIENTS FOR 28 CUBES
**Cake mixture from the Sacher Torte, p. 120**
**Butter and flour for baking tray · approx. 300 g puréed apricot jam
for spreading**

### FOR THE ICING
**300 g sugar · 180 ml water · 220 g chocolate · 2 Tbsps apricot jam**

### PREPARATION
Prepare the cake mix as for the Sacher Torte. Preheat the fan-forced oven at 200 °C. Grease a baking tray well with butter, and dust with flour. Shake off excess flour and spread the cake mix over an area of approximately 30 x 24 cm, and about 2 cm high. (Surround the edges of the mixture with aluminum foil folded twice or three times). Place in the oven and bake for 10–15 minutes. Remove and allow to cool.

Meanwhile, heat the puréed jam and stir until smooth. Thickly smooth the jam onto the cake with a spatula. Halve the cake horizontally and put together again with the jam side down. Immediately refrigerate (preferably put in the freezer) so the cake stays moist.

Cut the cake into cubes approximately 3 x 3 cm, first evening out the rough edges of the cake with a knife. Dip each of the cubes in the hot jam (or spread it over) and place on a cake grid. Allow to dry for an hour.

Meanwhile, heat up water and sugar for the glaze, letting it bubble for 5–6 minutes. Melt the chocolate over a double boiler, and stir gradually into the sugar water until a thick, smooth glaze is formed. Stir in the heated jam. Spread the glaze over the cubes and quickly smooth over with a spatula. Allow to dry, and serve in decorative paper cupcakes.

**BAKING TIME:** Approx. 10–15 minutes
**OVEN TEMPERATURE:** 200 °C in a fan-forced oven
**TIP:** This sweet treasure tastes best with whipped cream

# SACHER FASCHINGSKRAPFEN
# (Carnival Doughnuts)

**INGREDIENTS for approx. 16 closed doughnuts**
**330 g flour, fine · 80 ml milk · 30 g yeast · 1 egg · 3 egg yolks**
**pinch of salt · 40 g icing sugar · 1/2 pkt vanilla sugar · rind from 1 lemon**
**2 cl rum · 80 g butter · apricot jam with a little rum for the filling**
**flour for the work surface · vegetable oil, peanut oil preferred**
**Icing sugar for dusting**

**PREPARATION**

Warm up about 2 tablespoons of milk to drinking temperature and dissolve the yeast in it. Stir in a little flour to create a thick-pasted pre-dough. Sprinkle with flour, cover with a cloth and leave to rise in a warm place (28–30 °C) for about 15 minutes, until the surface begins to show small cracks.

Use the rest of the milk and stir together the egg, egg yolks, salt, icing sugar, vanilla sugar, grated lemon rind and rum. Add the melted butter and beat. Using a blender with a kneading hook, blend the mass with the remaining flour and the yeast dough until smooth. Cover with a cloth and leave to rise at room temperature for about 1 hour.

Knead the dough again and on a floured surface shape into a roll. Cut nut-size pieces about 20 g in weight and, using the palm of your hand, shape into round balls. Dust with flour and press them a little with a baking tray. Place on a baking tray and leave to rise in a warm place.

Heat some oil (160 °C) in a pan for deep frying or in a saucepan and fry a golden brown on both sides. Scoop out and place on a cake grid to drain. Fill a pastry bag with the rum-jam mix and squeeze into the doughnuts. Dust with icing sugar.

# VANILLA KIPFERL
## (Crescent-Shaped Vanilla Cookies)

### INGREDIENTS

**300 g flour, fine · 80 g icing sugar · pinch of salt · 80 g walnuts, peeled and ground · 2 egg yolks · 200 g butter, cold · pulp from 1 vanilla pod 100 g icing sugar for tossing · flour for the work surface**

### PREPARATION

Combine the flour, icing sugar, ground walnuts and salt, and heap onto a baking tray. Make a shallow hole in the middle and beat in the egg yolk.

Place small pieces of butter around the edge of the flour. Cut them into smaller pieces and, then with cold hands, quickly knead the mass into a smooth dough. (It is quicker and easier to use a blender). Shape the dough into a ball and cover with plastic wrap. Refrigerate for about 30 minutes.

Preheat the oven to 170 °C. Form small, finger-width rolls out of the dough and cut pieces about 1 cm thick from them. Roll into small balls and, on a lightly-floured surface, shape into crescents. Place on a baking tray lined with baking paper and bake for 12–15 minutes.

Loosen the crescents from the paper with a spatula, allow to cool, then toss them in the vanilla icing sugar. Allow to cool on a cake grid and then put into a cookie tin.

**BAKING TIME:** 12–15 minutes
**OVEN TEMPERATURE:** 170 °C

## "A GOOD BOY"

*An elderly American lady, who was staying at the Sacher "incognito", was very popular with the Sacher waiters for her friendliness. She talked to the personnel about their families, and found out from head waiter Herbert Müller that he was very proud of his "two good, well-behaved boys".*

*"My boys are also good," she said, not without pride. "One of them works for the American government."*

*When she had checked out, Müller asked who the kind lady had been. She was none other than Rose Kennedy, and her "good boy" working for the government was no less than the then President of the United States, John F. Kennedy.*

# WARM DESSERTS

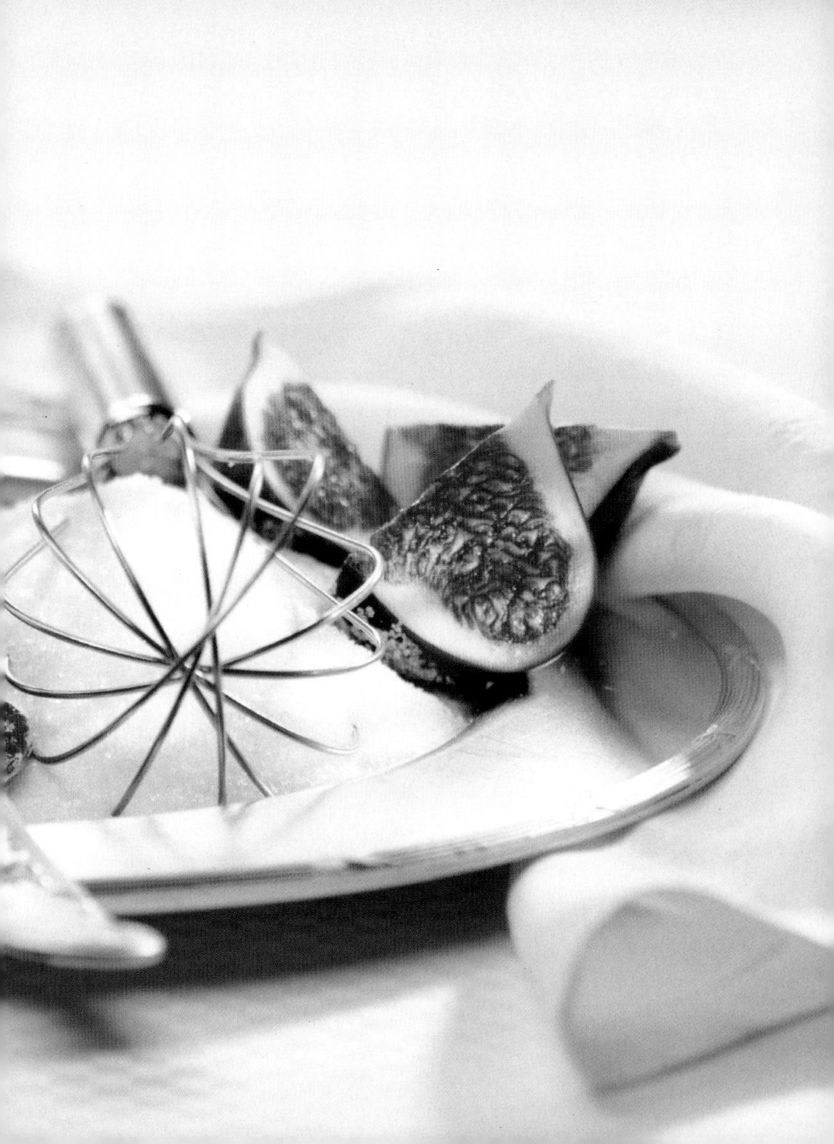

*Sacher*

# PLUM JAM TURNOVERS

## INGREDIENTS

**300 ml milk · 2 Tbsps butter · approx. 150 g flour, fine · 2 egg yolks
pinch of salt · flour for the work surface · 150 g plum jam, with
2 cl rum or plum schnapps, stirred · icing sugar**

## FOR THE BUTTER CRUMBS

**100 g butter · 100 g breadcrumbs · 50 g walnuts, ground
pinch of cinnamon · 2 Tbsp sugar · 1 Tbsp vanilla sugar**

## PREPARATION

Boil the milk with the butter and a pinch of salt. On low heat, stir in the flour
and keep stirring until a very smooth batter is formed. Transfer into a mixing bowl
and quickly mix in the egg yolks. Place the dough on a floured bread board and

allow to cool. Dust the dough with flour and roll out to about 2mm thick on a floured surface. With a round cutter, cut 12 shapes about 8 cm in diameter and brush the edges with water. Spoon small portions of the rum-plum jam mixture a little off-center of the dough cuts. Fold over from the sides without jam and firmly press the edges together.

Boil some water with salt and place the turnovers in the water. Simmer on low heat for about 5 minutes. Meanwhile, melt the butter for the butter crumbs in a pan and fry the crumbs, nuts, vanilla and sugar until golden brown.

Remove the turnovers from the water with a draining spoon and let drain. Toss them in the butter crumbs.

Serve the turnovers sprinkled with sugar.

**COOKING TIME:** Approx. 5 minutes
**SUGGESTED SIDE DISH:** Plum sauce (see Kaiserschmarren, p. 153)
**TIP:** Plum turnovers can be frozen and prepared by being boiled in bubbling hot water when needed.

 WARM DESSERTS

# POPPY SEED NOODLES

## INGREDIENTS FOR 6–8 SERVINGS

**500 g floury potatoes · 40 g butter · 100 g flour · 50 g semolina**
**50 g cornstarch (Maizena) · 100 g curd cheese (20 % fat) · 1 egg**
**1 egg yolk · Nutmeg, ground · salt · flour and semolina for the**
**work surface**

## FOR THE POPPY SEED CRUMBS

**150 g poppy seeds, finely ground · 80 g butter · 4 cl rum**
**4 Tbsps icing sugar · 2 Tbsps bread crumbs · icing sugar for dusting**

## PREPARATION

Peel the potatoes and boil in lightly salted water. Let them cool a little and then put through a potato ricer while still warm. On a work surface, combine the potatoes with the butter, flour, cornstarch, cottage cheese, egg, egg yolk, semolina, salt and nutmeg, and work into a smooth, elastic dough. Form a 3 cm thick roll, and using a cutter, cut out pieces about a thumb thickness wide. On a floured surface, make small noodles out of the dough.

Place on a baking tray sprinkled with semolina. Line a large cooking pot with baking paper and leave some paper for covering. Fill the pot with water, bring to boil and put the noodles in. Cover the water with baking paper and simmer, lightly bubbling, for about 5 minutes. (This way, the noodles stay under water and won't stick together). Remove with a draining spoon and let drain.

For the poppy seed crumbs, froth up the butter and combine with the rest of the ingredients. Toss the noodles well in the mixture. Serve on warmed plates and sprinkle with icing sugar.

**COOKING TIME:** Approx. 5 minutes

# TOPFENKNÖDEL
## (Curd Cheese Dumplings)

INGREDIENTS

**300 g curd cheese (20 % fat), pushed through a sieve · 60 g butter, melted · 60 g cubed white bread rolls · 2 eggs · 3 Tbsps sour cream 80 g semolina · pinch of salt · rind and juice from 1/2 lemon 1 Tbsp vanilla sugar**

FOR THE SUGAR CRUMBING

**100 g butter · 2 Tbsps vanilla sugar · 100 g breadcrumbs pinch of cinnamon powder**

PREPARATION

Combine well the melted butter and the white bread cubes, and mix in the rest of the ingredients thoroughly. Refrigerate for 2 hours.

Form 12 large dumplings from the mass and simmer in lightly boiling water for 8 minutes. Remove from the pot and let drain on kitchen paper. Toss in sugared breadcrumbs and arrange on a warmed plate.

For the sugared breadcrumbs, melt butter in a large pan. Add the breadcrumbs and fry a golden brown. Mix in the vanilla sugar and cinnamon. If desired, roast in the oven at 170 °C.

**COOKING TIME:** Approx. 8 minutes

*Sacher*

# APRICOT DUMPLINGS
# FROM THE WACHAU

## INGREDIENTS FOR 12 DUMPLINGS

**3 egg yolk · 3 egg whites · 120 g butter · 150 g fine semolina
150 g flour · 500 g curd cheese (20 % fat), pushed through a sieve
pulp from 1 vanilla pod · pinch of salt · 4 cl apricot brandy and
2 Tbsps sugar for the cooking water**

## FOR THE FILLING

**12 small, ripe apricots · 12 almonds, whole, peeled and roasted
80 g marzipan, mixed with Amaretto**

## FOR BUTTER CRUMBS

**150 g butter · 60 g sugar · 20 g vanilla sugar · 300 g breadcrumbs
Optional cinnamon · icing sugar for dusting**

## PREPARATION

For the dumplings, whip the butter until fluffy. First add the egg yolks then
gradually fold in the semolina, egg whites, vanilla pulp and a pinch of salt. Alternately, add the flour and curd cheese, stirring until a smooth dough is formed.
Make a roll out of the dough, wrap in plastic wrap, and leave to rise for about
1 hour.

Press the stones out of the apricots without cutting them. Into the cavity of each,
push in one almond wrapped in marzipan. Cut the dough into 12 slices and flatten
a little. Place one apricot on each piece. Wrap the fruit in the dough and form
smooth dumplings.

Boil some water in a large pot with a pinch of salt, sugar and the apricot brandy.
Place the dumplings in boiling water, then turn down the heat and simmer for about
20 minutes until they expand.

Meanwhile, heat some butter in a pan and fry the sugar, vanilla sugar and crumbs
on low heat until golden brown, stirring regularly. Add an optional pinch of
cinnamon. Remove the dumplings, drain well and carefully toss them in the
crumbs.

Prepare the dumplings for serving with the rest of the crumbs from the pan and
sprinkle with icing sugar. Serve quickly, while still hot.

**COOKING TIME:** Approx. 20 minutes

# "WHY ARE WE SO HAPPY TODAY?"

*The aristocracy has always loved the Sacher Hotel.*

*Head waiter Rudolf Reisinger recalls: "Above all, we've had many elderly, widowed countesses as our guests. Some only came for coffee and cake, others came regularly for lunch or dinner."*

*Today, Reisinger particularly remembers one elderly lady. "If you saw her on the street, you would have thought she was a normal little old lady. But as soon as she entered the hotel her eyes lit up. She'd then go to the Red Bar and would talk and joke with the likes of us.*

*"One day she looked at me and asked, 'Why are you smiling? Why are you in such a good mood?'"*

*One couldn't deny the old lady's sense of human nature. On that day, Rudolf Reisinger had become a father.*

# BOHEMIAN PLUM JAM LIWANZEN
## (Small, Fried Yeast Pancakes)

INGREDIENTS FOR 6–8 LIWANZEN

**20 g butter, melted · 15 g yeast · 20 g sugar for the pre-dough**
**180 ml milk, lukewarm · 130 g flour, fine · 2 egg yolks · 2 egg whites**
**100 g butter · 100 g plum jam · 100 g sugar for caramelizing**
**Pulp from 1/2 vanilla pod · rind from 1/2 lemon, grated**
**Icing sugar for dusting · pinch of salt**

**PREPARATION**

Dissolve the yeast, sugar and salt in the lukewarm milk. Stir in the sifted flour, making sure the batter is smooth. Then add the egg yolks, vanilla pod, lemon rind and melted butter. Cover, and leave to rise for 1 hour at room temperature. Whisk the egg whites until stiff and fold into the batter.

In a liwanzen pan (cast iron frying pan with round hollows), heat the butter and pour the batter into the hollows. (If you don't have a liwanzen pan, use metal rings about 6 cm Ø in a teflon-lined pan). Shake the pan so that the batter is evenly spread. Allow the liwanzen to cook for about 5 minutes on one side, turn over and finish cooking.

Remove, and brush half of the liwanzen with plum jam and sandwich with one without jam.

Caramelize the sugar in a pan, and dribble over the liwanzen. Serve dusted with icing sugar.

**COOKING TIME:** 8–10 minutes

# BUCHTELN (Baked Yeast Buns) WITH VANILLA SAUCE

## INGREDIENTS
**100 ml milk · 250 g flour, fine · 35 g sugar · 10 g yeast
40 g soft butter · 2 egg yolks · salt · rind from 1/2 lemon, grated
flour for the work surface · melted butter · icing sugar for dusting**

### FOR THE VANILLA SAUCE
**3 egg yolks · 150 ml milk · 125 ml cream · 60 g sugar
1/2 vanilla pod, cut open**

## PREPARATION
Prepare a sponge with lukewarm milk, yeast and 1/3 of the flour. Dust with a little flour and cover with a cloth. Leave to rise in a warm place. Then add the rest of the flour, sugar, egg yolks, lemon rind a pinch of salt. Knead into a semi-stiff dough. Finally, work in some butter. Cover with a cloth and leave to rise again until the bulk has increased considerably.

On a floured surface, roll the dough flat to about 2 cm. With a cutter, cut out pieces about 6 cm in diameter, fold and close the edges tightly at the top. Dip each piece one by one in the melted butter and place them closely side-by-side in a well-greased baking tray with the folded edge facing down. Bake in a preheated oven at 180 °C for about 20–30 minutes until golden yellow. Separate them to serve, and sprinkle over icing sugar.

For the vanilla sauce, heat the milk and vanilla pod. Simmer for about 5 minutes. Beat the egg whites and sugar. Gradually stir in the milk (without the vanilla pod) and keep stirring on medium heat until the sauce thickens slightly. Place the pot in a bowl filled with iced water and allow to cool, stirring now and again. When the sauce is cold, fold in some whipped cream.

**BAKING TIME:** 20–30 minutes
**OVEN TEMPERATURE:** 180 °C

# SCHLOSSERBUBEN (Prune Fritters)

## INGREDIENTS

**16 juicy prunes, pitted · 250 ml apple juice · 4 cl old plum brandy or rum
For the milk batter, 150 ml milk, 2 egg yolks · 2 whipped egg whites
30 ml oil · 1 cooking spoon vanilla sugar · pinch of salt · 100 g flour, fine
25 g sugar · 100 g marzipan · 3 cl plum brandy for the marzipan filling
100 g bitter chocolate, grated · 40 g icing sugar · butter or peanut oil
for baking**

## PREPARATION

Soak the pitted prunes in the apple juice and plum brandy over night. Pour off the
liquid, and drain on kitchen paper.

For the filling, mix well the marzipan and the plum brandy and fill into a pastry bag (round nozzle). Squeeze the mass into the cavity of the plums. Combine the grated chocolate with the icing sugar.

For the milk batter, combine 2/3 of the milk with the egg yolks, oil, vanilla sugar and salt. Add the flour and stir until smooth. Pour in the rest of the milk. Whisk the egg whites with the sugar until stiff and gently fold into the batter. Avoid stirring for too long, otherwise the mixture will become too thick.

Heat enough butter or oil for frying in a deep pan. Dip the plums in the mixture and fry a golden brown. Remove and drain well. Sprinkle with chocolate icing sugar.

SUGGESTED SIDE DISH: Vanilla sauce (see Buchteln, p. 146) or vanilla ice cream

# TOPFENPALATSCHINKEN
(Curd Cheese Crêpes)

## INGREDIENTS
75 g flour, fine · approx. 125 ml milk · 1–2 eggs · 2 1/2 Tbsps oil
rind from 1/2 lemon, grated · 1/2 tsps vanilla sugar · salt
oil or butter for frying · butter for greasing

## FOR THE CURD CHEESE FILLING
3 egg yolks · 3 egg whites · rind from 1/2 lemon, grated
200 g curd cheese (20 % fat), passed through a sieve · 60 g butter
40 g icing sugar · 1 tsp vanilla sugar · 2 tsp vanilla custard powder
salt · 60 g raisins, soaked in rum · 50 g sugar

## FOR THE SAUCE
125 ml milk · 125 ml sour cream · 2 eggs · 30 g icing sugar
1 tsp vanilla sugar

## PREPARATION
For the crêpes, combine the flour with milk, eggs and oil and stir. Add the lemon rind, vanilla sugar and a pinch of salt. Gradually add the rest of the milk and keep stirring until the mixture becomes thin. Put the batter through a sieve, and let stand for 20 minutes. If necessary, thin the mixture with more milk.

Heat oil in a pan suitable for making crêpes. Pour out any residual fat (the pancakes should be fried in a thin layer of oil). Pour in some of the batter, making sure it is evenly spread. Fry the crêpe golden yellow on both sides. Remove and place on a plate. Cover with foil. Make the rest of the crêpes in this way.

For the filling, beat the butter, icing sugar, vanilla sugar, custard powder, salt and lemon rind until fluffy. Gradually stir in the egg yolks and then the curd cheese. Beat the egg whites with the sugar until stiff and fold together with the raisins into the curd cheese mixture.

Place the crêpes in a row so that they overlap and become one connected piece. Spread over the curd cheese mixture and roll into one long roll. Cut the roll into 10 pieces. Grease an ovenproof dish with butter. Place the crêpes in the dish so that they are stacked on top of each other. Bake in a preheated oven at 160 °C for 15 minutes.

For the sauce, combine all the ingredients and stir until the mixture is smooth. Pour over the crêpes, and bake for another 15 minutes.

**BAKING TIME:** 30 minutes
**OVEN TEMPERATURE:** 160 °C

# MILCHRAHM STRUDEL
## (Milk and Curd Cheese Strudel)

FOR THE PASTRY (OR USE READY-MADE PASTRY)
250 g flour, fine · pinch of salt · 1 Tbsp oil · 2 Tbsps melted butter
for daubing · approx. 125 ml water, lukewarm · 2 egg yolks for daubing
icing sugar for dusting · Oil · flour for the work surface
butter for daubing

FOR THE FILLING
8 pieces of toast, without crust · approx. 125 ml milk · pulp from
1 vanilla pod · 60 g butter · 60 g icing sugar · 1 cooking spoon
vanilla sugar · rind from 1/2 lemon, grated · 3 egg yolks
250 g curd cheese · (20 % fat), passed through a sieve · 150 g sour cream
3 egg whites · 1 Tbsp sugar · 40 g raisins soaked in rum · 1 handful
almond splinters, roasted

FOR THE SAUCE
500 ml milk · 2 Tbsps sugar · 1 egg

PREPARATION

For the pastry, heap some flour onto a work surface and knead the pastry ingredients into a smooth, elastic dough. Shape into a ball and place in a soup bowl
dribbled with oil. Cover, and refrigerate, preferably over night.

On a lightly floured surface, roll out the pastry dough into a square with a rolling
pin. Pull until very thin. To do this, make sure your hands are covered in flour,
place one hand under the dough and use the other hand to carefully pull the
dough out from the center. The dough should become so thin that it's almost
transparent.

For the filling, heat up the milk with the vanilla pulp. Cut the toast into small cubes
and pour over the vanilla milk. Beat the butter, icing sugar, vanilla sugar, lemon rind
and egg yolks until creamy. Add the curd cheese and sour cream.

Beat the egg whites until stiff, gradually sprinkling in the sugar. Fold the soaked
bread into the egg yolk mixture. Finally, loosely fold in the egg whites.

Brush the pastry dough with butter and sprinkle over the almond splinters. Spread
the filling mixture over about 2/3 of the pastry and sprinkle the raisins evenly over
the top. Roll into a strudel. Place the strudel on a greased baking tray and brush
with beaten egg yolk.

For the sauce, whisk together all the ingredients and pour about a third of it over the strudel. Bake in a preheated oven at 180 °C for 40–50 minutes. While it's baking, regularly pour over the milk mixture and brush with melted butter.
Slice to serve and dust with icing sugar.

**BAKING TIME:** 40-50 minutes
**OVEN TEMPERATURE:** 180 °C
**SUGGESTED SIDE DISHES:**
Vanilla sauce (see Buchteln, p. 146)

# APPLE STRUDEL

### INGREDIENTS
**Strudel pastry as for the curd cheese strudel (see page 151) or use ready-made pastry · 1.5 kg apples (Elstar or other similar type) juice from 1 lemon · 60 g raisins soaked in rum · 200 g melted butter 100 g sugar · 2 Tbsps vanilla sugar · 100 g bread crumbs pinch of cinnamon powder · butter for daubing · icing sugar for dusting · 1 egg for daubing**

### PREPARATION
Prepare the pastry as for the curd cheese strudel. Peel and seed the apples. Slice into very thin slices. Dribble over some lemon juice.
In a bowl, combine 2 tablespoons of raisins and 1 tablespoon of vanilla sugar.
Brush the pastry dough with half of the melted butter, using the rest of the butter to fry the breadcrumbs. Combine the crumbs with the rest of the vanilla sugar and cinnamon and sprinkle over the pastry. Distribute the apples evenly over the pastry. Roll with the help of a dish towel. Make sure the ends are well closed. Place the strudel on a greased baking tray. (If the tray is too small, bend the strudel into a horseshoe shape).
Brush with the beaten egg and bake in a preheated oven at 180 °C for 30–40 minutes, occasionally brushing with melted butter.
When done, let the strudel cool, and dust with icing sugar. The strudel can be served either warm or cold.

**BAKING TIME:** 30–40 minutes
**OVEN TEMPERATURE:** 180 °C
**SERVING SUGGESTION:** With warm vanilla sauce or whipped cream

# KAISERSCHMARREN
# (Shredded Pancakes) WITH PLUM SAUCE

## INGREDIENTS FOR THE KAISERSCHMARREN

250 ml milk · 6 egg whites · 6 egg yolks · 130 g flour, fine
2 Tbsps sugar · shot of rum · 1 Tbsp vanilla sugar · lemon juice
2 Tbsps raisins · pinch of salt · normal sugar and icing sugar for dusting
butter for baking

## INGREDIENTS FOR THE PLUM SAUCE

500 g plums, small and firm · 100 g sugar · 100 ml red wine
Pinch of cinnamon · orange peel from 1/2 an orange, cut in large strips
juice from 1 lemon

## PREPARATION OF THE KAISERSCHMARREN

Beat the egg whites and sugar in a bowl until stiff. In another bowl, combine
the milk, flour, egg yolks, lemon juice, rum, vanilla sugar and salt. Stir until batter
is smooth. Fold in the egg whites.

In a large ovenproof pan, heat some butter and pour in the batter. First brown on
the stove, then turn over and bake both sides until brown in a preheated oven at
180 °C. Take the pan out of the oven and, using 2 forks, break the mass into small
pieces. Mix in the raisins, sprinkle with sugar and put into the oven again until the
sugar is caramelized.

Serve with icing sugar.

**COOKING TIME:** 8–10 minutes
**OVEN TEMPERATURE:** 200 °C

## PREPARATION OF THE PLUM SAUCE

Halve and pit the plums. Caramelize the sugar, then pour over the red wine.
Simmer until the liquid is reduced by half. Add a pinch of cinnamon, the orange
peel and simmer for 8–10 minutes. Add lemon juice to taste, and remove the
orange peel. Allow to cool.

**COOKING TIME:** 8–10 minutes

# SALZBURGER NOCKERLN, WITH OR WITHOUT?

*In order to compensate for the fact that they are not allowed to drink wine, members of the Saudi Arabian royal house often excessively indulged in eating desserts, recalls Jaroslav Müller, Sacher's long-time head chef.*

*As well as the Sacher Torte, the esteemed guests particularly enjoyed the Salzburger Nockerln (fluffy egg soufflé).*

*"For the foreign guests we served the Salzburger Nockerln with cranberries because in our experience this was better received," recalls Müller.*

*One Saudi Arabian prince who was used to this practice was once mistakenly served the dessert without cranberries. "Where's the ketchup today?" he asked, dumbfounded.*

## SALZBURGER NOCKERLN
## (Fluffy Egg Soufflé)

### INGREDIENTS

150 ml milk · 1/2 vanilla pod · squeeze of lemon juice · 7 egg whites, cooled
pinch of salt · 80 g sugar · 4 egg yolks · rind from 1 lemon, grated
10 g vanilla sugar · 2 Tbsps flour · 1 Tbsp cornstarch (Maizena)
icing sugar for dusting · butter for greasing

### PREPARATION

Heat the milk with the cut-open vanilla pod and lemon juice. Remove from the stove and leave to sit. Remove the pod. Smear an oval-shaped, ovenproof form with butter and pour in enough vanilla milk to cover the bottom.

With a hand mixer, mix the cooled egg whites with a pinch of salt and a third of the sugar until very stiff. Slowly add the rest of the sugar and continue to beat until the mixture is thick and creamy.

Preheat the oven on 220 °C. Add the egg yolks, lemon rind, vanilla sugar, flour and

cornstarch to the egg white mixture and fold three or four times with a whisk (the mass shouldn't become homogenous). Make 4 pyramid-shaped nockerl, placing them next to each other in the baking tray. Bake for 10–12 minutes until light, golden brown.

Dust with icing sugar and serve quickly so the nockerl don't collapse.

**BAKING TIME:** 10–12 minutes
**OVEN TEMPERATURE:** 220 °C
**TIPS:** To add a fruity taste, bake on a bed of cranberries.
To make sure all the residual fat is removed from the bowl in which the eggs are whisked, simply rub the bowl with lemon juice.

# MOHR IM HEMD
## (Chocolate Hazelnut Pudding)

50 g bittersweet couverture or cooking chocolate · 30 g icing sugar
3 egg yolks · 3 egg whites · 3 cl rum · 2 Tbsps sugar · 50 g breadcrumbs
50 g crumbed ladyfingers · 2 Tbsps milk · 50 g hazelnuts or walnuts,
roasted and grated · pinch of salt · approx. 100 g melted butter for
greasing · 3 Tbsps sugar for the baking forms

FOR THE CHOCOLATE SAUCE
150 g dark chocolate · 150 ml milk · 20 g sugar · 100 ml cream
1/2 vanilla pod, cut open · 80 g soft butter · 1 cl cognac
300 ml half-whipped cream for decoration

PREPARATION
Grease some small soufflé molds with melted butter and dust with sugar. Refrigerate (so that the mixture can rise without running over the sides). Melt the chocolate in a double boiler.

Whisk the egg yolks with rum and icing sugar until fluffy. Pour in the melted chocolate. Whisk the egg whites and sugar and a pinch of salt until half stiff and carefully fold in about 1/3 of the egg whites.

Combine the breadcrumbs, ladyfinger crumbs and milk and fold into the mixture, along with the nuts and the rest of the egg whites.

Fill the molds 3/4 full with the mixture. Fill a deep baking tray with about 2 cm of water (or use a double boiler) and place the molds in the water. Bake in a preheated oven at 170 °C for about 20 minutes.

For the chocolate sauce, heat the milk with the cream, sugar and vanilla pod. Remove the vanilla pod and melt the finely chopped chocolate in the mixture. Whip up the butter and pour in the chocolate mixture, stirring regularly. Pour in some cognac for extra aroma.

Loosen the small cakes from their molds and arrange on plates. Pour on the warm chocolate sauce, and decorate with whipped cream.

BAKING TIME: Approx. 20 minutes
OVEN TEMPERATURE: 170 °C
SUGGESTED SERVING OPTIONS: Vanilla or pistachio ice cream, strawberry sauce and hippen (a type of thin wafer)

## HOTEL SACHER GUESTS

*As well as the famous tablecloth that Anna Sacher had signed by prominence during the emperor's rule, including the emperor himself, the Sacher also has a "normal guestbook", whose signatures provide exciting reading.*

*Here are only some of the prominent guests who have stayed in the Sacher Hotel:*

*Anna Netrebko · Astrid Lindgren · Caroline von Monaco · Christian Thielemann Edita Gruberova · Franz Welser-Möst · Gabriele Schnaut · Grace Bumbry Grace Kelly · Günther Krämer · Jean Cocteau · John Neumayer · John Travolta · José Carreras · Jürgen Flimm · Queen Elizabeth II · Queen Beatrix of the Netherlands · Luc Bondy · Nelson Mandela · Peter Simonischek · Peter O'Toole · Placido Domingo · Oscar Straus · Romano Prodi · Robert and Einzi Stolz · Shah Reza Pahlevi and wife Soraya · Sean Connery · Thomas Hampson Tobias Moretti · Uderzo · Uschi Glas · Vaclav Havel · Vera Kalman · Vesselina Kasarova*

# IMPORTANT INFORMATION

*Measurements of dry ingredients in American, British and Australian recipes are usually listed by volume. European recipes on the other hand, are measured by weight. Below is a conversion table for your convenience.*

*Weighing the ingredients with a kitchen scale is recommended, as this will improve the final result.*

*The following conversions may be useful:*

*1 ounce = 28,35 g · 1 g = 0,035 ounces*
*10 ounces = 283,5 g · 100 g = 3,5 ounces*

*1 US cup = 237 milliliters (ml)*
*1 UK, Australian or Canadian cup = 250 ml*

*1 standard US Tablespoon (Tbsp) = 15 ml*
*1 standard UK Tbsp = 15 ml*
*1 standard Australian Tbsp = 20 ml*
*1 standard Canadian Tbsp = 15 ml*

*Teaspoons (Tsp) can be converted 1:1*

*All recipes yield 4 servings.*

# INDEX

Apple Strudel  152
Apple-Horseradish Sauce  106
Apricot Chutney  40
Apricot Dumplings from the Wachau  142
Apricot Filling  40
Asparagus, Oven, from the Marchfeld  70
Asparagus, White, Dressed in Ham  31

Backhendl à la Anna Sacher
  (Fried breaded chicken )  86
Beef Roulade  106
Beef Soup, Classic Viennese  44
Bohemian Carp in Dark Beer  80
Bohemian Mushroom Goulash  69
Bohemian Plum Jam Liwanzen
  (Small, Fried Yeast Pancakes)  145
Boiled Beef (Tafelspitz)
  with Classic Side Dishes  105
Bread Dumplings  52
Breast of Veal, Stuffed, Viennese Style  101
Brioches, Butter  30
Buchteln (Baked Yeast Buns)
  with Vanilla Sauce  146
Buns, Baked Yeast (Buchteln),
  with Vanilla Sauce  146
Butter Brioches  30
Butter Crumbs  138, 142

Cabbage, Red  91
Cabbage-Pasta Bake (Krautfleckerl), Classic  74
Cake, Plum, with Hazelnut Crumble  131
Cardinal Slices  129
Carnival Doughnuts
  (Faschingskrapfen), Sacher  134
Carp, in Dark Beer, Bohemian  80
Carp, Styrian, with Root Vegetables
  and Caraway Seed Potatoes  78
Chestnut-Potato Dumplings  93
Chicken, Fried Breaded,
  (Backhendl à la Anna Sacher)  86
Chicken Paprika  88
Chicken Soup, Old-Style Viennese  49
Chive Sauce  72, 106
Chocolate Cream  127
Chocolate Hazelnut Pudding
  (Mohr im Hemd)  157

Chocolate Sauce  157
Chutney, Apricot  40
Classic Krautfleckerl
  (Cabbage-Pasta Bake)  74
Classic Viennese Beef Soup  44
Cookies, Crescent-Shaped, Vanilla
  (Vanilla Kipferl)  135
Cream, Chocolate  127
Cream, Vanilla  127
Cream Slices  132
Creamy Viennese Veal Goulash
  with Dumplings  55
Crêpes, Curd Cheese
  (Topfenpalatschinken)  149
Crêpes Slivers  46
Crumbing, Sugar  141
Crumbing, Walnut  91
Crumble, Hazelnut  131
Crumbs, Butter  138, 142
Crumbs, Poppy Seed  140
Cubes, Sacher  133
Curd Cheese Crêpes
  (Topfenpalatschinken)  149
Curd Cheese Dumplings  141

Dough, Pasta  65, 75
Doughnuts, Carnival
  (Faschingskrapfen), Sacher  134
Duck, Free-Range, with
  Semolina Dumplings and
  Red Cabbage and Quince  90
Dumplings  55
Dumplings, Apricot,
  from the Wachau  142
Dumplings, Bread  52
Dumplings, Chestnut-Potato  93
Dumplings, Curd Cheese  141
Dumplings, Egg  71
Dumplings, Semolina  46, 91
Dumplings, Veal Liver  47

Egg Dumplings (Eiernockerln)  71
Eggs, Fried, with Truffles
  and Potato Fritters  26
Eiernockerln (Egg Dumplings)  71
Esterházy Torte  125

Faschingskrapfen
   (Carnival Doughnuts), Sacher 134
Fiaker Goulash with Sacher Sausages 34
Filling, Apricot 40
Fluffy Egg Soufflé
   (Salzburger Nockerln) 155
Free-Range Duck with
   Semolina Dumplings and
   Red Cabbage and Quince 90
Fried Breaded Chicken
   (Backhendl à la Anna Sacher) 86
Fried Eggs with Truffles and Potato Fritters 26
Fried Onions 107
Fried Potatoes 106, 108
Fried Veal Liver, Viennese Style 102
Fried Watermelon with
   Smoked Sheep's Cheese 68
Frittaten 46
Fritters, Porcini-Potato,
   with Lamb's Lettuce 72
Fritters, Prune (Schlosserbuben) 148

Gherkin Mustard 108
Goose-Liver Cake, Original Sacher 40
Goulash, Creamy Viennese Veal,
   with Dumplings 55
Goulash, Fiaker, with Sacher Sausages 34
Goulash, Szegediner 56
Goulash, Viennese 54
Gugelhupf, Marble 120

"Ham Pasta" (Schinkenfleckerl)
   Covered with Baked Cheese 59
Hazelnut Crumble 131

Ice Wine Jelly 40

Jelly, Ice Wine 40

Kaiserschmarren (Shredded Pancakes)
   with Plum Sauce 153
Krautfleckerl (Cabbage-Pasta Bake),
   Classic 74

Lamb, Roast, in a Potato Fritter Jacket
   (Rösti) 114
Lamb's Lettuce 38, 72
Liwanzen (Small, Fried Yeast Pancakes),
   Bohemian Plum Jam 145

Malakov Chocolate Torte 127
Marble Gugelhupf 120
Meat with Rice (Reisfleisch),
   Sacher-Style 57
Milchrahm Strudel
   (Milk and Curd Cheese Strudel) 151
Milk and Curd Cheese Strudel
   (Milchrahm Strudel) 151
Minced Veal Butter Schnitzels 102
Mohr im Hemd
   (Chocolate Hazelnut Pudding) 157
Mushroom Goulash, Bohemian 69
Mustard, Gherkin 108

Noodles, Poppy Seed 140

Old-Style Viennese Chicken Soup 49
Old-Style Viennese Salon Beuschel
   with Bread Dumplings 52
Old Viennese-Style Roast Pork
   with Fried Potatoes 112
Onion Quiche "Sacher Eck" 62
Onions, Fried 107
Original Sacher Goose-Liver Cake 40
Oven Asparagus from the Marchfeld 70

Pancakes, Shredded (Kaiserschmarren),
   with Plum Sauce 153
Pancakes, Small, Fried Yeast (Liwanzen),
   Bohemian Plum Jam 145
Paprika Chicken 88
Paprikas, Stuffed, Sacher-Style 60
Pasta Dough 65, 75
Pheasant Wrapped in Bacon
   with Chestnut-Potato Dumplings 93
Pike-Perch, Serbian 83
Plum Cake with Hazelnut Crumble 131
Plum Jam Turnovers 138
Plum Sauce 153
Poppy Seed Crumbs 140
Poppy Seed Noodles 140
Porcini-Potato Fritters with
   Lamb's Lettuce 72
Pork, Roast, Old Viennese Style,
   with Fried Potatoes 112
Potato Pouches with Truffles 75
Potato Soup, Viennese 48
Potatoes, Fried 106, 108
Prune Fritters (Schlosserbuben) 148

Pudding, Chocolate Hazelnut
    (Mohr im Hemd) 157

Quiche, Onion, "Sacher-Eck" 62
Quince 91

Red Cabbage 91
Reisfleisch (Meat with Rice), Sacher-Style 57
Roast Lamb in a Potato Fritter Jacket
    (Rösti) 114
Roast Pork, Old Viennese-Style,
    with Fried Potatoes 112

Sacher Cubes 133
Sacher Faschingskrapfen
    (Carnival Doughnuts) 134
Sacher Rolls with Mushroom
    and Tafelspitz Spread 32
Sacher-Style Reisfleisch (Meat with Rice) 57
Sacher Tafelspitz Aspic with
    Lamb's Lettuce 38
Sacher Torte 120
Salon Beuschel, Old-Style Viennese,
    with Bread Dumplings 52
Salzburger Nockerln (Fluffy Egg Soufflé) 155
Sauce, Apple-Horseradish 106
Sauce, Chive 72, 106
Sauce, Chocolate 157
Sauce, Plum 153
Sauce, Vanilla 146
Schinkenfleckerl ("Ham Pasta")
    Covered with Baked Cheese 59
Schlosserbuben (Prune Fritters) 148
Schnitzel, Wiener 98
Schnitzels, Minced Veal Butter 102
Semolina Dumplings 46, 91
Serbian Pike-Perch 83
Shredded Pancakes (Kaiserschmarren)
    with Plum Sauce 153
Sirloin à la Esterházy 110
Sirloin with Onions, Fried Potatoes
    and Cherkin Mustard 108
Slices, Cardinal 129
Slices, Cream 155
Soufflé, Fluffy Egg
    (Salzburger Nockerln) 155
Strudel, Apple 152
Strudel, Milchrahm
    (Milk and Curd Cheese Strudel) 151

Strudel, Milk and Curd Cheese
    (Milchrahm Strudel) 151
Stuffed Breast of Veal,
    Viennese Style 101
Stuffed Paprikas, Sacher-Style 60
Stuffed Veal Kidney Roast 100
Styrian Carp with Root Vegetables
    and Caraway Seed Potatoes 78
Sugar Crumbing 141
Swiss Roll 130
Szegediner Goulash 56

Tafelspitz Aspic, Sacher,
    with Lamb's Lettuce 38
Tafelspitz (Boiled Beef)
    with Classic Side Dishes 105
Topfenknödel
    (Curd Cheese Dumplings) 141
Topfenpalatschinken
    (Curd Cheese Crêpes) 149
Torte, Esterházy 125
Torte, Malakov Chocolate 127
Torte, Sacher 120
"Trout Quartet" with Freshwater Trout,
    Noodles, Spinach and Trout Caviar 65
Turnovers, Plum Jam 138

Vanilla Cookies, Crescent-Shaped
    (Vanilla Kipferl) 135
Vanilla Cream 127
Vanilla Kipferl
    (Crescent-Shaped Vanilla Cookies) 135
Vanilla Sauce 146
Veal Butter Schnitzels, Minced 102
Veal Goulash, Creamy Viennese,
    with Dumplings 55
Veal Kidney Roast, Stuffed 100
Veal Liver, Fried, Viennese Style 102
Veal Liver Dumplings 47
Venison with Rowan Berries
    and Chestnut Pear 116
Viennese Goulash 54
Viennese Potato Soup 48

Walnut Crumbing 91
Watermelon, Fried, with
    Smoked Sheep's Cheese 68
White Asparagus Dressed in Ham 31
Wiener Schnitzel 98